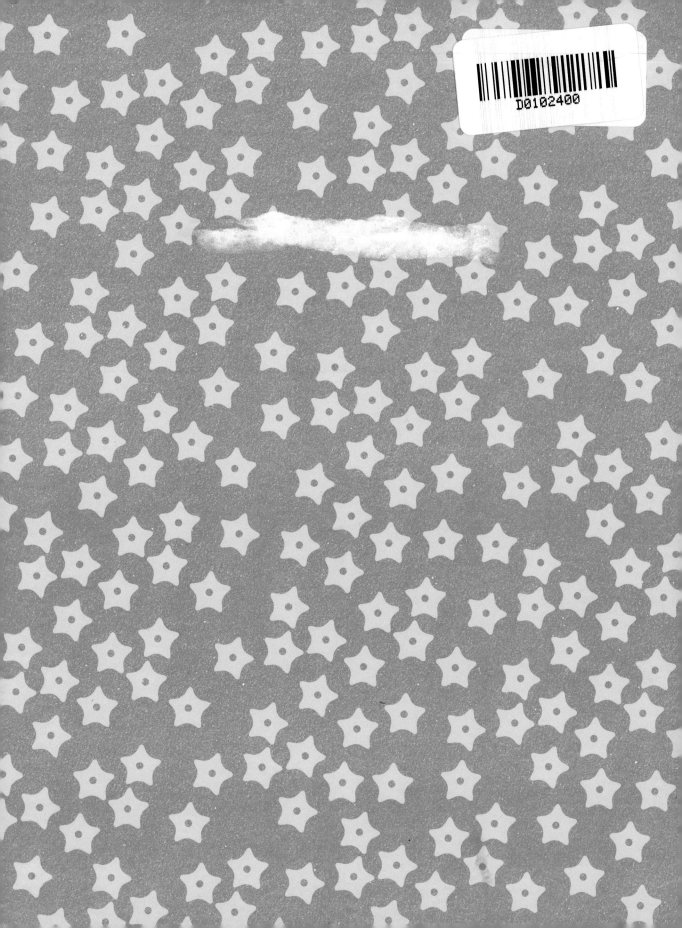

for may and billy

first published in great britain 2012

bloomsbury publishing plc,
50 bedford square, london wc1b 3dp
bloomsbury publishing, london,
berlin, new york and sydney

a cip catalogue record for this book
is available from the british library

isbn 978 1 4088 0180 2

designer and illustrator: georgia vaux
photographer: jill mead
indexer: hilary bird

10 9 8 7 6 5 4 3 2 1

printed and bound in china

all papers used by bloomsbury publishing
are natural, recyclable products made
from wood grown in well-managed forests.
the manufacturing processes conform
to the environmental regulations of the
country of origin.

www.bloomsbury.com/joannaweinberg

cooking for real life

joanna weinberg

photography by jill mead

BLOOMSBURY

LONDON · BERLIN · NEW YORK · SYDNEY

there are so many types of cookbooks. In a funny way, they reflect all the sorts of friendships you can have. There are friends you look to for sharing dark times, and those who are better on sunnier days. There are showy ones, whose gang you want to be part of but know you never quite will. There are the ones that you fall in love with, urgently, passionately, seeking only their company for weeks on end, and the slightly boring ones, who you can always depend on to be there for you. Sometimes, you know exactly who it is you want to spend time with; at other lonelier times, no one can quite fill the need. Over time, some slip away, taking off in a different direction, while others walk the same road, and you grow closer still.

When I began to cook in my early twenties, I wanted a gentle guiding hand to show me how to get good food onto the table. Nothing challenging or complicated. I was nervous of recipes, fearful that if I departed from them in any way at all, disaster would unfold, and I would not get to eat. So I decided not to cook from them directly – if I wasn't following instructions, I couldn't get them wrong. Instead, I read them at bedtime: little stories that would seep into my head and allow me to recreate them in an unstressed dream sequence.

Over time, as with everything else in life, what I wanted from my cookbooks changed. With increasing confidence, I began to embrace recipes. I wanted variety, adventure: to learn about different ingredients and flavours from all over the world. I was ready to step up to some methods, too: how to make pastry, meringues, mayonnaise – the sort of cooking that only chefs or mothers could do. The bookshelf began to buckle and groan. People who knew more about food and cooking than me (and there are many) urged me towards the classics: Elizabeth David, Claudia Roden, Marcella Hazan – to see where it all began, to know where it came from, and from them to develop my own taste and style.

It helped that at that time I was living in California, writing for magazines. I had few friends, little to do in my spare time, and access to some of the best and most varied produce you could dream of. I read, and played with food, and cooked a lot for myself – no one else seemed to eat much in LA.

So, when I came back home, to clouds and rain and dark-early evenings, to a proper kitchen that I loved and to friends I loved even more, I flexed my new kitchen muscles, and set about cooking for them. It was my way of re-establishing friendship after years abroad. The cookbook I wanted then was one that showed me how to cook for others without it causing untold stress and formality. I couldn't find such a book, so I wrote it instead, and it became *How to Feed Your Friends with Relish.*

Soon after, without my really noticing it, life grew up around me. Friends got married, bought homes, settled down. And so did I. Babies began to appear and the rhythms of friendship changed. Dinner out became rare; cocktail hour, extinct. I moved, with my new husband, across town, to a more buggy-friendly place. We bought a kitchen table, big enough to fit our new, messy life onto. Tiny pairs of shoes crept onto its surface, alongside the candlesticks and tea lights. Clearing it was a never-ending task; as soon as one end was done, the mess crept in again from the other. I finally felt like I was no longer waiting for life to happen to me. I was living it. This is what I mean by Real Life.

The fridge, for a start, is now more often full than empty. I make lists, and tick them off, too. My days are organised, timetabled even (well, relatively). I have discovered the marvels of cooking from my store cupboard, partly because the ingredients I have access to without forethought are quite limited, but mostly because I can't bank on being able to pop out at any given moment.

Like many people, the bulk of my shopping now takes place on the internet, which, while convenient, is not inspiring. Interesting ingredients need a day's notice; but we still need to eat today. It's a new way of thinking for me.

Time seems to have compacted. The space I had in my day for leafing through cookbooks to figure out what might be nice for supper has simply disappeared, like the last warm ray of summer. Mostly I'll be working out how to make my staples as varied and interesting as I can with as little effort as possible. This is as often something that can be prepared in advance and then left to take care of itself in the oven for an hour, as it is cook-and-slap-it-right-down kind of food. Either way, these days, I rarely cook anything that needs more than 15 or perhaps 20 minutes' attention.

So I rifle through my cookery shelf seeking a different kind of friendship now. What I want is a mucker, a book that rolls up its sleeves and wades into the daily drudge with a cheerful grin. A book that gives short shrift to the pretentious, that celebrates and reinvigorates the everyday. More than anything, I want it to inspire me. I need ideas – of course they should be fresh, seasonal, accessible – for the food I really want to eat. But even more importantly, I want ideas for the sort of food that I am able to cook now.

I couldn't find that book, so I set about writing it, and this is what it has become. It is the book I need now. I hope it's the one you do, too.

your kitchen

h ere's some good news. Much of the slog of being the daily cook can be done before you even pick up a knife. It's about getting your kitchen working for you, rather than you working in the kitchen.

This could well mean changing your attitude to, and relationship with, fresh and long-lasting ingredients. It's all very well being talented with fresh, seasonal ingredients, but most of us don't have access to them on a daily basis. Once the first flush of a trip to the market, shops, or weekly box is passed and you have gobbled the fresh food that needs eating soonest, you will return to the backbones of cooking: the longer lasting ingredients in your fridge, cupboard and freezer. Much comes down to how you think about, shop for and organise these.

What you want is to have up your sleeve a versatile, reliable and broad-reaching stock of provisions (not fancy or expensive) to see you through the week (and month and year), so that you're not having to rush back out to buy ever more food. The more you can explore and enjoy the food you have to hand, the more flexible, efficient and spontaneous your eating life becomes. And it all starts with how you shop.

shopping

No two words in the English language put greater fear into my heart than 'weekly shop'. To me, they spell everything wrong in the functioning of a happy kitchen. Every minute I spend in the supermarket, I feel like a little piece of me dies. Whether you hit the 'Buy Again' button online, or trawl the same old aisle for the same old products, season notwithstanding, you're likely to be consigning yourself to a narrow and repetitive cooking cycle.

The planned weekly shop may promise economy, but it tends to deliver waste. The get-one-free usually ends up in the bin, whilst meat bought a week ago with the intention of being supper tomorrow lingers sadly on the bottom shelf rather than being put immediately into the freezer, in the hope you'll still get to it before it goes off.

More than anything, it tends to mean meals planned to the extent that there is no room left for improvisation or spontaneity, the two characteristics of spirited and inspiring cooking. A 'bangers-and-mash because it's Tuesday' mentality may feed your body but it will never nourish your soul.

All this said – or ranted, rather – a household needs to function in a sensible, efficient way, and most importantly this means always having basics to hand, and having the tools to improvise on the occasions you don't. Much depends on your storage options. If you can find – or create – a cool, dark place to keep larger volumes of oils, dried, bottled and tinned goods, do so, you will need to shop for them less often. It doesn't matter where – it could be under the stairs or in the basement if you have one. If your bedroom cupboards are cool and dark, promote them; they have now become your larder. Having a well-stocked store cupboard is the key to a varied eating life.

Use the supermarket for what you need it for, and then look beyond its sliding doors. Think instead of how you'd really like to shop – in a French market perhaps, or a cobbled street of great independent shops – then mirror that online. Open up your shopping to amazing delicatessens, cheesemongers, butchers, organic fruit and vegetable producers and anything else you can dream of – yes, they need a day or two's notice, but that becomes a habit with surprisingly little practice.

So the internet has become my village. While I am not able to touch, sniff or taste produce before I buy it, I have got to know my providers on the phone – and they have got to know me. I will talk to the butcher about different cuts and cooking recommendations, or the deli about the best cheeses at any given time. Our box delivery schemes have a list of our 'likes and dislikes' to bear in mind. I trust them, I enjoy the shopping, and the packages and boxes that arrive in the post are a great source of pleasure.

To create your own perfect online village, ask around for recommendations from friends (mine are in the Directory in the back of the book, p.278). There's nothing like a regular customer to give you an honest lowdown. Behave as you would on any regular shopping trip: take time to browse, ring up with any questions, make requests, give feedback – like any good local shop, they'll want to provide the best for their regular customers.

Keep in mind that most organic box schemes have become more like general grocers. They are flexible and wide-ranging, allowing you to add to or top up your box with all sorts of other produce, not just with perishables (often including meat and delicatessen fare) but good quality imperishables, too. When deciding who to shop with check out delivery policies and schedules first. If they have a scheduled weekly delivery, for instance, you may prefer one that delivers in your area at the start rather than the end of the week. Check the costs, too – some are free, some you'll only want to use once you have built up a long enough list to make an order worthwhile.

organising your provisions

In much the same way that a tiny bookshop can have every book you have ever wanted to read, yet the largest can still be disappointing, a well-stocked kitchen is not about the amount of storage space you have but good management. There are broadly two kinds of provisions – the staples, which are your capsule wardrobe as it were, the jeans and little black dresses of the kitchen – reliable, adaptable, easily available (here I would include pasta, rice, pulses and the like). And then there are the transformative ingredients, which are the culinary equivalent of a dressing-up box and take the simple ingredients and lift them into something else entirely. These are more likely to come in glass jars or bottles: capers and cornichons, pink pickled ginger, anchovies etc. With the aid of these, in a heartbeat you can be in the hotly fragrant Middle East, or wearing mittens up a mountain. They are the fastest, cheapest way to the thrills the world holds when you don't have time even to poke your head out of the door.

Of both kinds there are endless options, so it's useful to know yourself as a cook before plunging into the bottomless choice. Most of us lean towards groups of flavours from distinct schools of cooking, whether the robust, rustic flavours of the southern Mediterranean, or the exotic fragrances that hail from further east. Once you can see where your strengths and preferences lie, you can kit yourself out, not with a vast array of provisions, but the right combination of ingredients to reflect your style of cooking.

Mentally, I break my shopping down into the three places that it ends up – the freezer (as it needs unpacking first), then the fridge, and finally the trusty store cupboard.

the freezer

It is not very groovy to use a freezer. Fashion would have us meandering down to the farmers' market, butcher and grocer on a daily basis. But in reality, to run a busy life, to eat well at home and to have what you need when you need it, a freezer is a life saver.

One of the great fallacies of the freezer is that you are suspending animation. In fact, everything continues to deteriorate, just in a different way, and at a different pace. If you know you're going to freeze something, do so on the day of purchase, otherwise you will always regard it with suspicion. To keep food in the best possible nick, it needs to be well wrapped and labelled so you can recognise it later, including the date. If it's not, you will find freezer burn marks – the dark spots normally crowned in an icy frost that may appear on

food which is too exposed. It's harmless, but ugly. Proper freezer bags, plastic lidded airtight containers or even rinsed-out plastic milk bottles (for soup and stock) all work well as freezer packaging. To maximise your space, keep any containers as evenly sized and shaped as you can; square and oblong are best. For energy efficiency, squeeze as much air out as possible, leaving just a little headspace, as it will expand a bit, and keep your freezer full – even if it's just with bags of ice. If you are freezing a large amount, turn down the freezer to its coldest setting for 24 hours so that the unfrozen food will not raise the temperature in the freezer. Thaw, if you possibly can, in the fridge. The food will deteriorate much less if it defrosts slowly.

meat in the freezer
Meat, more than anything, continues to deteriorate in the freezer. It makes sense, then, to avoid freezing the better cuts if you possibly can – that juiciness in a fillet or tenderloin is what the cut is all about; enjoy it while it is fresh.

The length of time you can freeze meat for differs: most meat can be deep frozen for six to twelve months (halve this for fatty meat such as bacon and sausages) if it is well wrapped, but fridge-freezers tend to be less effective, so that time should be halved. Most supermarket packaging is not sturdy enough to prevent damage over time in the freezer, so double wrap. Butchers will do this properly for you if you tell them something is for the freezer.

fish in the freezer
Fish copes less well in the freezer than meat unless properly prepared, so think of it as the most temporary of homes. If you want to freeze fish you have caught, it needs to be ready to cook before it goes in – gutted, descaled, and filleted, if that is the final intention. Crab and lobster meat should be cooked first.

dairy in the freezer
Some dairy produce, like cream, freezes reasonably well – at least to use for cooking purposes. Milk needs to be thawed slowly in the fridge or it will separate. Don't judge it until it has completely thawed; it may split as it defrosts, but have faith, it will probably come together at the last moment with a good shake. Once defrosted, it needs to be used within a day or two.

The only cheese I find worth freezing is freshly grated Parmesan, which can be used directly on pasta, and saves those few extra, precious seconds when children are impatient with hunger and on the verge of meltdown.

the fridge

It's hard to imagine what life would be like without a fridge. It's as instrumental to daily cooking as the stove. Like all of us, it has its strengths and weaknesses. It allows us the freedom to shop less often, to enjoy leftovers for longer, to trust that the food we eat will be in good condition. As with any friend, the more you know and understand their behavioural traits, the better you will enjoy their company.

The fridge is a cold place with a very specific microclimate. It will dry out meat and cheese, which need to be well wrapped in clingfilm to keep them moist. Oil-based sauces and dips like pesto will dry out too, and need a preventative slick of oil over their surfaces. It will strangely have the opposite effect on cooked pastry – there's no trick to get over soggy pastry, better to leave it out of the fridge and eat it within a day.

Many vegetables last a very long time in the fridge – and while it is preferable to have vegetables crunchily delicious, that half bunch of celery that so often seems to linger limply in the fridge will still do its bit in soups and stocks, and many hard veg (leeks, carrots, cauliflower to name a few) last much longer than the marked use-by dates anticipate. Once salad leaves are released from their plastic prisons, they need to be guzzled quickly. Organic perishables tend to last for less time than non-organic, so by the end of the week it can all feel a bit patchy.

A fridge has a strange habit of appearing to fill itself up; it seems at times that the more you eat from it, the fuller it gets – there's always a stray piece of ham, some lost-looking yoghurt or the back end of a large cauliflower to navigate. Without wanting to state the very obvious, it's worth thinking about what will go off fastest when deciding what to cook. Somehow you need to strike a balance between enjoying produce when it's at its freshest but still eating that which will go off the fastest, to avoid having to throw things away.

Which brings us to leftovers. Often, they are the greatest treat of all – many people enjoy Boxing Day far more than the Christmas feast, for that reason. Wrap and label them clearly, and keep in mind that the clock is ticking against them. Try using them differently to the first time around to prevent everyone's eyes glazing with boredom. Know your bottom-feeder – if they pass over something, sure as toast no one else will eat it, so it's time for it to go.

the store cupboard

The store cupboard is mostly for the foot soldiers of cooking – pasta, rice, tinned goods. But the smaller bottles, jars and tins that also inhabit these shelves are the ones that bring delight and surprise, like anchovies, capers, soy sauce, sesame oil and rosewater.

We all consume ingredients at different rates. There are always gaps, as well as bottles that have stayed long after they're welcome. Sometimes you can get around this with alternatives; at others, only that one ingredient will do. It's all too easy to allow experimental ingredients to clutter this valuable space, so they need a judicious prune, particularly at the change of the seasons, when our eating habits adapt to the weather. Sometimes this simply means moving bottles around in the cupboard for better access, as dry ingredients you use often will rarely reach their use-by date.

As well as moving things from front to back, and throwing out ingredients that never served their purpose, you will reacquaint yourself with bits and bobs you'd forgotten about: the pomegranate molasses that adds such tang and piquancy to stews, dressings and marinades, or the pickled Japanese ginger that can brighten any simple piece of meat, fish or salad.

However, it is well to remember that sell-by dates can be somewhat random and exist, as often as not, because manufacturers are obliged to put something down. They can generally be treated as very loose guidelines. Spices, however, particularly ground ones, once open, will lose their intensity after a few months. If you don't get that instant fragrant hit as you open them, discard and move on. It is worth keeping an eye on those old men baking powder and bicarbonate of soda, as their powers to rise may diminish with age.

Keep good oils and spices away from the stove and preferably the fridge too. They will spoil with the heat. All the goodness in fancy olive, nut and seed oils breaks down in heat, which is part of the reason there is no point in cooking with your good stuff. Decant small amounts to have readily available next to the stove, refresh them regularly, and keep the rest somewhere cool and dark. A note about garlic, the odd one out here: darkness and cold temperatures signal the winter and sprouting time, so it will keep best if it's warm and dry, imitating the long rest it has in the ground in the deep late heat of summer.

stocking up on provisions

Everyone has a slightly different idea of what are the essential provisions. While some motor through a variety of pulses, others will rely heavily on chopped tomatoes. Here you'll find a good spread of ingredients that should cover most everyday cooking situations. With a few extras and relatively little effort, magic can be made – starting with most of the recipes in this book.

If you ask around, you'll find most people have a 'secret ingredient' they like to add to almost everything, like a signature. The effect of these is substantial – a squeeze of lemon juice or a spoon of crème fraîche can be added to many of the same dishes with wildly differing results.

The asterisked ingredients listed here are the ones I rely on, either to form the basis of a dish, or to transform an everyday standard into something altogether more interesting. To find out just why they are my favourites, turn to the hall of fame (p.24).

freezer

Chicken stock*
Parmesan cheese, grated*
Sausages
A whole chicken if you can fit it in;
   a few thighs if you can't
Beef mince
Cooked, peeled North Atlantic prawns
Frozen spinach (preferably leaf)
Petits pois*

Good bread, sliced
Pitta bread
Vanilla ice cream
All-butter shortcrust pastry

fridge

Feta cheese*
Halloumi cheese
Butter
Double cream or crème fraîche
Plain yoghurt
Eggs
Bacon, lardons or cooking chorizo*
Celery
Carrots

Fresh pesto
Oily black olives
Dijon mustard*
Wholegrain mustard
Walnut oil

bottles, pickles, preserves and aromatics

Worcestershire sauce

Soy sauce

English mustard powder

Capers

Anchovies (fillets in olive oil) *

Cornichons

Tahini *

Pomegranate molasses *

Pickled ginger

Redcurrant jelly

White wine

Red wine

oils and vinegars

Extra virgin olive oil *

Vegetable or sunflower oil

Sesame oil

Herb oils: rosemary, basil and chilli

Sherry vinegar

White wine vinegar

nuts and fruits

Blanched almonds *

Walnuts

Pine nuts

Pumpkin seeds

Sunflower seeds

Sesame seeds

Dried apricots

Sultanas

Coconut milk

pasta, rice and pulses

Pasta (something long, eg spaghetti and something short, eg fusilli)

White rice (something long grain, eg basmati and something short grain, eg Arborio)

Wholegrain brown rice

Chickpeas *

Puy lentils, dried and cooked (vac-packed)

Cannellini beans, dried and tinned

larder staples

Flaky salt and black pepper

Onions

Garlic

Fresh lemons *

Tinned tomatoes

sweet things and baking

Plain flour

Strong white flour

Jumbo rolled oats

Bicarbonate of soda

Baking powder

Chocolate – 70% cocoa solids

Cocoa powder

Caster sugar

Muscovado sugar

Icing sugar

Fruit sugar or agave nectar

Golden syrup

Black treacle

Condensed milk

Vanilla extract

Digestive biscuits

Rosewater

*the hall of fame

These are the cooking stars of my kitchen, the characters that add depth and interest to so many simple dishes.

chicken stock

If I had to pick any ingredient for an Order of Merit, it would be fresh chicken stock. Everything about it is honest – it is almost free, for a start, using up nothing but leftovers or basics that need to be used anyway, plus a little of your time. And then it just gives and gives – to soups, risottos, stews, ragus. It never tastes the same but its contribution in flavour is priceless, because it makes everything taste homemade. It's also happy in the freezer for ages – make sure to label it, as it looks like a lot of other things once frozen.

I tend to stockpile chicken bones in the freezer until I have enough to make up a good batch of stock. You can make this recipe simpler still by omitting the carrots and celery, though you will lose the sweet roundness that vegetables add.

makes 1.5–2 litres

2 chicken carcasses, cooked or uncooked
3 onions, quartered
3 carrots, roughly chopped
2 sticks celery
2 bay leaves
6 whole peppercorns
Salt

Put all the ingredients into a large pan, cover with water and bring to the boil, skimming any scum off the surface. Reduce to the merest simmer, and cook for 2–5 hours, topping up with water every so often.

Strain and lightly season. If you want to freeze some and don't have much room in the freezer, boil to reduce by half, or even four times, making a note to reconstitute before using. Transfer to rigid plastic containers (I like to use rinsed-out plastic milk bottles), remembering to leave space for the stock to expand if you are going to freeze it. Allow to cool before refrigerating. And in turn, chill in the fridge before labelling, dating and freezing.

parmesan cheese

What I find most interesting about Parmesan is that it works on two levels: as an ingredient, and also as a seasoning. Grated, it functions as the latter, most obviously on top of pasta and risotto dishes, but it will sing, particularly in salads, in the form of larger curls and shavings. It lasts a long time well wrapped in the fridge, but for long-lasting, instant access, keep it grated in a tub in the freezer and help yourself to it directly from there.

petits pois

Everyone loves a little pea, and unless you are pulling them off the plant yourself, the frozen ones are far better quality than the so-called fresh ones. The trick to capturing their sweet flavour and fresh texture is to let them come not quite to a full boil, but drain them as soon as you see the water beginning to prickle.

feta cheese

Feta is a generous creature. Baked whole with oil and herbs it becomes an instant warm lunch; crumbled it adds substance to any salad, and tang and flavour to most pulses. Or simply smear on a crust and scatter with chopped olives to make a picnic fit for king or shepherd alike.

bacon

Bacon – and its relations pancetta, lardons and chorizo – is about as useful an ingredient imaginable to have in the fridge. Good old bacon rashers are the most flexible, whether in a sandwich, with eggs, laid across game, chopped into pasta, mince, lentils or soups – in fact almost anything will be improved by a hit of salty pork. If it is mostly to be used as a flavour enhancer, it's best to buy a chunk of smoked pancetta that you can cut bits off in whatever shape you choose, as it will be more flexible and last longer.

dijon mustard

If I had to choose any processed ingredient to celebrate, Dijon mustard would be top of my list. Its smoothness and rounded flavour make it the perfect choice to use as the base for salad dressings and mayonnaise, but no stew or Bolognese in my house gets away without a dollop of it, and neither a steak nor a ham sandwich would be the same without it.

anchovies
Anchovies punch well above their weight, packing loads of flavour into each tiny fillet. When fried, they disintegrate, leaving behind a vibrant smack of umami. Their great friends in the flavour world are garlic and chilli. A plea: seek out producers who are committed to sourcing them sustainably.

tahini
This paste made from ground sesame seeds is most commonly found in houmous. But it has a great versatility, and can be used thinned down and pulsed with herbs to make a delicious sauce for meat or salad dressings. Stir right to the bottom of the jar before using, as the oil rises to the surface.

pomegranate molasses
This sticky syrup made from highly reduced pomegranates is a regular character in Middle Eastern cooking, but has more friends up its sleeve. It adds piquancy to rich, meaty stews and pies, and tomato-based sauces and marinades.

extra virgin olive oil
There's little to add to the pantheon of praise for extra virgin olive oil. It is worth taste-testing a few varieties: the Italian oils are the royalty, and each region will bring its own nuance to the table. However, it burns at a relatively low temperature, so use basic olive oil for frying instead.

blanched almonds
Blanched almonds are found all over the place in cooking. They can be ground to use in cakes or curries, chopped to scatter over cereal or salads. I like to toast them with salt and rosemary, and eat warm with a glass of cold sherry.

chickpeas
Chickpeas are my favourite pulses. I use them in so many different ways: to add bulk to salads or stews, in curries, to replace breadcrumbs in meatballs, or just simply dressed with olive oil and lemon juice. The best are the large Spanish kind that come in glass jars.

fresh lemons
There are few dishes that can't be improved by a little squirt of lemon's freshness, or grating of its zest. Its juice is a seasoning, too, and can be used in place of salt.

the daily grind

superfood salad

Simmer quinoa in twice its volume of lightly salted water for 10 minutes, then switch off the heat and allow it to absorb the rest of the liquid. Toss with baby spinach, chopped avocado and feta or grilled halloumi, and dress with good olive oil and plenty of lemon juice. (If you have some leftover roast butternut squash to hand, it would be delicious here.)

a tray of crispy chicken joints

Turn chicken joints in olive oil, lemon juice and herbs or spices of your choice, eg ground ginger and coriander, sumac, thyme or oregano, and salt. Roast in a hot oven (200°C/gas 6) for 30–40 minutes, depending on the size of the portions. Breasts will take the least amount of time, so if you are mixing the joints, add them to the pan 5 minutes later. Eat with rice, broccoli or green salad and the pan juices.

spinach carbonara

Defrost the spinach (preferably leaf), squeeze dry and stir into a couple of egg yolks, with a dash of cream, salt, pepper and nutmeg. Cook your pasta, drain and toss very well with the egg and spinach mixture. Eat with generous amounts of grated Parmesan, salt and pepper.

pasta with chilli garlic breadcrumbs

Fry chopped garlic and dried chilli flakes in olive oil, until golden and scented. Add breadcrumbs, toss through evenly with the fragrant oil and toast in the pan until crunchy and coloured. Sprinkle over pasta loosened with a little olive oil and a spoon of cooking water, and scatter with plenty of grated Parmesan cheese and salt.

open halloumi sandwich

Rub good white toast (preferably sourdough) with garlic and olive oil. Top with slices of fried halloumi cheese, mint and rocket leaves and halved cherry tomatoes. Serve with a final drizzle of olive oil and freshly ground black pepper.

i n a perfectly cooked world, our kitchens would be full to the brim of seasonal vegetables, fragrant spices and growing herbs. We'd see great vistas of opportunity in our cupboard and enjoy infinite variety in our daily mealtimes. And without a second glance we'd be able to conjure up an original feast to sit down to at the family table every evening. But this is Real Life.

This chapter is about the sort of everyday cooking we all have to contend with: taking what is easily available to you and making it exciting. It's having that plate of pasta up your sleeve that could start a conversation, and a plan for chops that won't make you collapse with boredom.

It's also about spontaneity. No forethought should be required for everyday cooking. That means turning with confidence to what you already have in the cupboard, fridge and freezer and reacquainting yourself with some familiar ingredients. Teach them to play some new tricks and you'll be relieved of the scourge of endless scurrying to the shops.

The recipes here are grouped together in small handfuls around faithful fallbacks: chicken, sausages, chops, vegetables, soups, simple pasta dishes and fish. In each there are three or four different variations, to cover the surprising breadth that these simple ingredients can span. None of it is demanding cooking – they should all be easily within reach after a tiring day's work.

There is no reason that your everyday meals, reliable as they are, need to be a drudge. Like learning fresh dance moves with a lifelong partner, they are instead a chance to make the familiar new.

what to do with chicken pieces

chicken piri piri — This is a brilliant store-cupboard staple. You can make extra sauce to keep in the fridge for a month or so – great with prawns, pork fillet or white fish. I have purposely left the volume of chilli a bit vague as it really depends on how fiery your mood, or who you're cooking for. If you want to make it a little fancy, buy poussins from the butcher and ask for them to be spatchcocked: you can then either grill or barbecue.

feeds 4

6 plump garlic cloves
8 tablespoons olive oil
Juice of 1 lemon
2–3 fresh chillies, finely chopped, or
  2–3 dried bird's-eye chillies, crumbled
½ teaspoon cayenne pepper
2 teaspoons fresh chopped oregano
  or 1 teaspoon dried

4 large chicken thighs or leg joints
Sea salt
Good old green salad (p.271) and
  Perfect baked potatoes (p.272)
  or rice, to serve

Squash the garlic cloves under the blade of a knife and slip off the skin. Place the ingredients apart from the chicken and salt in a saucepan and simmer for 2–3 minutes.

Make a couple of slashes in the chicken skin (to allow the sauce to seep in), place in an ovenproof dish and pour the sauce over. Cover with foil and set aside to marinate for as long as you can – even 20 minutes will make a difference. Marinate at room temperature for up to 1 hour or in the fridge for more than 1 hour. Preheat the oven to 200°C/gas 6.

Cook for 15 minutes, then remove the foil, scatter with salt, increase the oven temperature to 220°C/gas 7 and cook for a further 20 minutes until the chicken skin is crisp and golden and the flesh is cooked through. Serve with salad and baked potatoes or rice, with the juices spooned generously over the top.

chicken and spinach rice

chicken and spinach rice — This is the very simplest of chicken and rice dishes: soothing to eat, undemanding to make and loved by all. I tend to use risotto rice as it gives exactly the right consistency – soft, yet still with bite – but any white rice will do.

feeds 4

4 chicken joints
Olive oil, for frying
1 good-quality chicken stock cube or
  900ml fresh stock
5 cubes frozen spinach or 300g fresh
  baby spinach leaves

1 small onion, finely chopped
120g risotto rice
1 heaped tablespoon crème fraîche
A few fresh basil leaves, torn
2 tablespoons finely grated Parmesan
Salt and freshly ground black pepper

Season the chicken with salt and pepper. In a little olive oil, brown the chicken well all over in a large sauté pan (this should take a good 10 minutes). If you are using a stock cube, dissolve it in 900ml boiling water. If you are using frozen spinach, defrost it by pouring over boiling water, set aside for 5 minutes, then strain off all the water.

Once the chicken is golden, set it aside, pouring off any extra fat. Deglaze the pan with a little stock, scraping up all the delicious caramelised bits and returning the liquid to the jug of stock.

Wipe out the pan, add a little more olive oil and gently sweat the onion until soft and translucent. Return the chicken to the pan, with the rice and most of the stock. Bring to a simmer and cook gently for 15 minutes.

Add the spinach, pushing it into the hot liquid, and simmer for a further 5 minutes. Check from time to time you have enough liquid, adding extra stock or water if it looks like it is drying out – you want the finished dish to have a gentle, soupy consistency.

When the rice is tender, remove the pan from the heat. Stir in the crème fraîche and scatter with the torn basil, Parmesan and salt and pepper. I like to serve this in soup bowls.

anchovy and oregano chicken and chips — This is a

simple store-cupboard supper, almost instant to assemble and deliciously salty and satisfying. If you prefer to eat chicken breast you will only need one each; buy them with the skin and bone, and reduce the cooking time by 5 minutes.

feeds 4

10–12 anchovy fillets in olive oil,
    drained
5 tablespoons olive oil
2 tablespoons dried oregano
2 large or 3 medium garlic cloves,
    finely chopped

2 large or 3 medium potatoes
4 chicken leg joints
Freshly ground black pepper
Sautéed spinach (p.270) or Good
    old green salad (p.271), to serve

Preheat the oven to 220°C/gas 7.

Mash the anchovies into the oil and mix in the oregano, garlic and plenty of black pepper. Put into a large ovenproof pan or roasting tin. Cut the potatoes into 1cm chips (no need to peel), and toss thoroughly in the mixture.

Add the chicken pieces and rub the mixture in, patting large bits of anchovy into the skin. Lay the chicken in the centre of the tin and spread the chips around the edge. Put in the oven and cook for 35–40 minutes, tossing the chips once halfway through so that they colour evenly.

Remove the chicken once golden and crunchy, and the juices run clear when the thickest part of the leg is pierced with a knife. Set aside to rest for 5 minutes. Return the chips to the oven for a final blast of colour if necessary. Eat with sautéed spinach, or just a green salad.

sausages three ways

sausages with fennel and onion gravy – This is an old
favourite, and the addition of the fennel gives it a more subtly sophisticated
flavour – but you could double the onions instead.

feeds 4

1 medium onion, peeled but
  left whole
1 large fennel bulb, left whole
Olive oil, for frying
1 tablespoon fennel seeds

Pinch dried chilli flakes (optional)
8–12 sausages
1 large glass medium sherry or Marsala
Smooth mash (p.272), to serve

Preheat the oven to 190°C/gas 5.

Shave the root off the onion and fennel so the bulbs still hold together. Quarter
the onion and fennel and then cut the quarters in half to give you 8 wedges of
fennel and 8 of onion.

Heat a little oil with the fennel seeds and chilli flakes, if you are using them,
in a large roasting tin set over a medium heat. Add the onion and fennel to the
pan, turning frequently to colour all over – beware burning, because the tin is
comparatively thin compared to a frying pan; this could happen very quickly.

Once the vegetables are lightly coloured all over, add the sausages to the tin,
turning to coat in the oil, and then add the sherry or Marsala. You want the
liquid to come about half way up the sausages. Transfer to the oven and roast
for 40 minutes, turning every so often until the sausages are deep brown all over,
and the onions and fennel are soft and sweet. You may want to top up the liquid
with water, making sure it doesn't dry out and burn, as you should have enough
at the end to use as a generous gravy. Serve with plenty of mash.

rigatoni with sausage ragu

rigatoni with sausage ragu – It's always useful to keep sausages in the freezer. Skin them and they become endlessly versatile. If you're sharing with kids who don't like strong flavours, omit two of the garlic cloves and the herbs. Soften them separately in olive oil and mix into your portion before adding to your pasta.

feeds 4

Olive oil, for frying
1 medium onion, chopped
8 good-quality sausages, herby if you can
   get them
3 medium garlic cloves, finely chopped
1 small glass white wine
1 tablespoon finely chopped fresh
   rosemary leaves or 1 teaspoon dried

1 tablespoon finely chopped fresh sage
   or 1 teaspoon dried
400g tin chopped tomatoes
100ml double cream (optional)
400g rigatoni
Salt and freshly ground black pepper
Grated Parmesan, to serve

Preheat the oven to 180°C/gas 4.

Warm a good glug of olive oil in a large flameproof casserole and fry the onion gently for 15 minutes, so that it softens and begins to turn golden. Meanwhile, heat 1 tablespoon of olive oil in a frying pan, squeeze the sausages out of their skins and begin to fry, breaking up the meat so it looks like mince. Allow it to turn golden on one side before flipping it over and continuing to break up. When the meat is coloured right through, about 10 minutes, add it, along with its juices, to the casserole, add the garlic and fry for a few minutes.

Meanwhile deglaze the frying pan with the white wine, scraping out all the tasty caramelised bits into the casserole. Add the herbs, stir around, bubbling off the wine, and then add the tomatoes. Cover, bring to a simmer and transfer to the oven for 30 minutes. Season to taste and stir in the cream, if using.

Cook the rigatoni in plenty of boiling water (well salted if you're not sharing with very young children) according to the packet instructions. Toss the drained pasta into the casserole, stir well to coat in the sauce and scatter with plenty of fresh Parmesan, to serve.

sausage with chilli and purple sprouting broccoli

This is amazingly flavourful despite its simplicity. The key is to make it in a large sauté pan so that you have plenty of room to break up the sausages and that they can properly fry. If the pan is too crammed, they will steam instead. If purple sprouting is not in season use tenderstem or calabrese broccoli broken up into slim florets instead.

You need only serve this with yoghurt or crème fraîche and crusty bread, though mash would work well, too, if you have the spirit to make it.

feeds 4

2 tablespoons olive oil
Scant teaspoon dried chilli flakes
3 medium garlic cloves, finely chopped
1½ teaspoons fennel seeds, bashed
650g good-quality pork sausagemeat (or sausages, squeezed out of their skins)

600g purple sprouting broccoli, chopped a little
Juice of 1 lemon
Flaky salt
Greek yoghurt or crème fraîche and crusty bread (p.247), to serve

Heat the oil in a large frying pan and fry the chilli, garlic and fennel seeds until the garlic is golden and all is fragrant.

Crumble in the sausagemeat, turning it well in the mixture, and breaking it up to form mince. Then leave it to cook so that the bottom becomes golden and well coloured. Turn the meat and break it up again and cook on the other side until well coloured.

Meanwhile, blanch the broccoli for 1 minute in boiling, salted water, then drain. When, and only when, the meat is well coloured, add the broccoli, turning it well to coat in the oil. Add the lemon juice, partly cover and leave to cook for 5 minutes, stirring and turning from time to time. The broccoli will still be fairly crunchy but this adds to its appeal.

Stir again to check everything is evenly cooked, scrunch over salt, then divide between plates and eat immediately, with a dollop of yoghurt or crème fraîche and plenty of good bread.

three ways with chops

pork chops with creamy mustard and pink ginger

This is an excellent standby, the pickles cutting through the creamy mustardy
sauce and perfectly offsetting the simple but savoury chops. I like it with rice
and sautéed spinach, though you could also stir the crème fraîche and mustard
through the spinach, for a tart take on creamed spinach.

feeds 4

4 thick pork chops
4 tablespoons crème fraîche
1 heaped tablespoon wholegrain mustard
½ teaspoon white wine vinegar

Salt and freshly ground black pepper
Pink pickled Japanese ginger or finely
  sliced cornichons
Rice and Sautéed spinach (p.270), to serve

Preheat the grill to high.

Season the chops well and grill until just cooked through but still juicy,
6–8 minutes on each side.

Stir together the crème fraîche, mustard and white wine vinegar, to serve as
a sauce alongside. Arrange the chops on plates along with a neat pile of pink
pickled ginger or finely sliced cornichons. Serve with rice and sautéed spinach.

everyday lamb chops — There are few more simply pleasing suppers than a succulent, sizzling lamb chop. If you're low on basic aromatics, and have some kind of herb, chilli or garlic oil, this is the place to use it. I like this with white bean purée, but if you fancy something a little more interesting, serve the chops with minted tahini sauce or salsa verde.

feeds 4

2 plump garlic cloves, peeled
Leaves from 2 rosemary sprigs
8 anchovy fillets in olive oil, drained
1 teaspoon olive oil (herb, chilli or garlic
  if you have it)

4 good-sized lamb chops
Freshly ground black pepper
White bean purée (p.270), Minted tahini
  sauce (p.273) or Salsa verde (p.273),
  to serve

Preheat the grill to high.

Pound the garlic, with the rosemary leaves and anchovies, until you have a rough paste. Add the olive oil and smear the paste all over the chops. Season with black pepper, and grill on each side for 6–8 minutes until sizzling golden outside and juicy and just pink within.

Serve with mash and broccoli and the sauce of your choice.

roast lamb chops with butternut and figs

roast lamb chops with butternut and figs – If you want to speed this dish up, you can buy prepared bags of cubed sweet potato and butternut flesh which work just as well. Or if you find the idea of butternut too sweet, you could cube potatoes into 1cm pieces instead.

As an alternative to the preserved lemon, you could use the pared zest of an unwaxed lemon, cut into small pieces.

feeds 4

4 good-sized lamb chops
1 small butternut squash, deseeded and
   cut into 2cm cubes
1 preserved lemon, chopped
1 head garlic, broken up but not peeled
Olive oil, for drizzling

Good squeeze of lemon juice
1 heaped teaspoon ground cumin
½ teaspoon ground chilli (optional)
4 figs
Salt and freshly ground black pepper

Preheat the oven to 200°C/gas 6.

Place the chops, butternut, chopped preserved lemon and whole garlic cloves in a large roasting tin. Coat everything in a slick of olive oil, squeeze over the lemon juice, and sprinkle with the cumin and chilli, if using. Finally, season well and roast in the oven for 20 minutes.

Meanwhile, prepare the figs by making a cross in the top to about half way down. After 20 minutes of cooking, turn the chops and toss the butternut around so that it's not sticking and burning. Place the figs in the tin, drizzling with some of the juices, and return to the oven for a further 10 minutes before serving.

three satisfying vegetable dishes

gado gado — This warm Indonesian salad makes a delicious corner-shop supper to throw together with whatever vegetables are to hand. Incidentally, the peanut sauce is equally delicious with chicken, beef or prawns, and will happily keep, sealed, in the fridge for a few weeks.

feeds 4

4 eggs
800g French beans, topped, or any
  crunchy green vegetables
1 tablespoon chopped fresh coriander
  leaves
White rice and soy sauce, to serve

for the peanut dressing:
1 garlic clove, chopped
2 small shallots, chopped
1 tablespoon vegetable or groundnut oil
¼ teaspoon hot chilli powder
½ teaspoon dark brown sugar
1 tablespoon dark soy sauce
125g crunchy peanut butter
Juice of ½ lemon
Salt

First make the peanut dressing. Crush the garlic and shallots in a mortar with a little salt. Heat the oil in a small pan and fry the garlic and shallot paste for a couple of minutes, so that it softens without colouring. Add the chilli, sugar, soy sauce and 250ml water, and bring to the boil, then add the peanut butter. Simmer for about 10 minutes, stirring occasionally, until the sauce thickens. Add the lemon juice and more water if necessary until you have to the consistency of double cream, then set aside.

When ready to eat, place the eggs in a small pan of water, bring to the boil and cook for 7–8 minutes; they should not be quite hard-boiled. Hold the eggs under running water until cool enough to handle, then peel and quarter them.

Cook the beans in a pan of boiling water until tender but still with bite – about 5–6 minutes. Warm up the sauce again, and in a bowl toss thoroughly through the beans then lay the eggs on top. Scatter with fresh coriander and serve with lots of white rice and soy sauce.

vegetable pilaf – This is a perfect one-pot curry, and one of the rare ones that isn't sloppy. It's substantial enough to eat on its own, but you could eat it as a side dish alongside grilled chicken or chops or the Spiced pollack (p.72).

feeds 4

1.5 litres vegetable stock
240g basmati rice
40g butter
1 tablespoon vegetable oil
2 small or 1 large onion, finely chopped
250g cauliflower, broken into florets
75g cashew nuts
½ teaspoon ground cumin
1 teaspoon ground coriander
¼ teaspoon ground cardamom
¼ teaspoon ground turmeric

¼ teaspoon hot chilli powder
Pinch saffron threads
100g frozen peas
100g tinned, drained chickpeas
2 tablespoons chopped fresh
   coriander leaves

for the raita:
Pinch ground cumin
250g plain yoghurt
10cm piece cucumber, grated
Salt

Bring the vegetable stock to the boil, add the rice and boil vigorously for 5 minutes. Drain and set aside.

In a large pan melt the butter and oil together over a fairly high heat, and fry the onion until turning golden. Add a pinch of salt, the cauliflower, cashews, cumin, ground coriander, cardamom, turmeric, chilli and saffron. Fry for a couple of minutes, turning so that everything is well coated in oil and spices.

Push the vegetable mixture into a mound in the middle of the pan. Stir the peas and chickpeas through the rice and pack the mixture around and on top of the vegetables and nuts. Pour over 325ml boiling water. Wrap the lid of the pan in a tea towel, and place on the pan so that no steam can escape. Set over a high heat for 3–4 minutes. Reduce to a low heat and steam for 10–12 minutes until the water is absorbed. Switch off the heat and allow to rest for 1–2 minutes.

Remove the lid, lay a plate upside down over the pan and invert both in one movement, so that the rice lands on the plate with the vegetables and nuts on top. Scatter over the coriander leaves.

To make the raita, stir a good pinch of salt and the ground cumin into the yoghurt and mix in the cucumber. Either spoon over the rice, or serve on the side.

ed's warm salad

ed's warm salad — My husband, Ed, makes this salad – it's comforting without being heavy, wonderfully easy and couldn't be tastier. For carnivores, a handful or two of lardons thrown in with the mushrooms never goes amiss.

feeds 4

4 small beetroot
1 red onion, peeled and cut into 8 wedges
Olive oil, for drizzling and frying
150g green beans, topped
4 portobello mushrooms, thickly sliced
1 garlic clove, chopped
2 knobs of butter
1 block halloumi cheese, cut into
   5mm slices
150g rocket
75g pine nuts (lightly toasted if you
   can be bothered)

Small bunch flat-leaf parsley, chopped
Handful of tarragon, mint, dill, chervil,
   chives, or any other soft herbs
Salt and freshly ground black pepper
Crusty bread (p.247), to serve

for the dressing:
4 tablespoons extra virgin olive oil
1 tablespoon sherry vinegar
Good squeeze of lemon juice

Preheat the oven to 180°C/gas 4.

Toss the beetroot and onions in oil in a roasting tin, scatter over salt, and roast for 40 minutes, or until the beetroot is tender.

Meanwhile cook the beans in boiling salted water for 5–6 minutes, until tender but with some bite. In a frying pan, fry the mushrooms and garlic in the butter and a little olive oil, until golden and tender, and set aside. Wipe out the pan to nearly dry and fry the halloumi on both sides until golden and softening. Remove and set aside.

To make the dressing, combine the extra virgin olive oil, sherry vinegar and a generous squeeze of lemon juice in a small jug, and stir well to combine.

Add the dressing to the frying pan and warm it through. Peel the beetroot and cut into quarters, and put into a salad bowl, along with the onions, beans, mushrooms, garlic, halloumi and rocket. Pour over the warm dressing and toss well. Scatter with the pine nuts, fresh herbs and salt and pepper. Eat immediately with lots of good crusty bread.

three things on toast

st john rarebit — St John is my favourite restaurant. They do English food better than anyone, in my opinion. I love their version of cheese on toast, for its salty strength and mustardy kick. For the very best results the cheese needs to be cooled and set for at least an hour until it is thickly spreadable and holds together on the toast.

feeds 4

Knob of butter
1 tablespoon plain flour
1 teaspoon English mustard powder
½ teaspoon cayenne pepper

200ml Guinness
Generous dash of Worcestershire sauce
450g mature Cheddar cheese
4 x 1cm-thick slices bread

Melt the butter in a small pan, stir in the flour, and cook together until it smells biscuity but is not browning. Add the mustard powder and cayenne pepper and then stir in the Guinness and Worcestershire sauce, allowing it to bubble away gently for 5–10 minutes, stirring to prevent sticking, to cook out the flour.

Stir the cheese into the flour mixture until it is melted. When it's smooth, remove from the heat, pour it into a shallow container, and allow to cool and set for at least 1 hour in the fridge.

When you are ready to cook, preheat the grill to high and toast the bread on both sides. Spread the cheese mixture on the toast and grill for 5 minutes or so, until bubbling and brown.

garlic chard with egg and bacon – This lip-smackingly tasty number is most often a dish I'd make just for me, but here it is scaled up for four in case you're feeling generous enough to share. The trick to take away from this recipe is the stress-free method of poaching eggs, which a friend in the trade taught me. With this method, you can poach in the sort of numbers at the same time you wouldn't dream of doing free hand. I prefer to use chard in this as it's a bit more substantial than spinach, but it's not always available, in which case spinach will work fine.

feeds 4

4–8 eggs, depending on your hunger
8 rashers streaky bacon or 200g lardons
4 garlic cloves
1kg fresh chard, chopped if the leaves are large, stalks trimmed and cut into 2cm lengths

2 tablespoons olive oil
4 large slices white bread, preferably sourdough
Butter, for spreading
Salt and freshly ground black pepper

First, prepare the eggs. Break each into a good-sized square of clingfilm so that you can twist the ends together to seal into a little, transparent package – like a goldfish from the fair but without the air pocket.

Bring 5cm of water to a whispering simmer in a sauté pan or saucepan. Meanwhile, cut the bacon rashers into strips about 1cm wide (I find scissors are best for this). Slice the garlic very thinly. Rinse the leaves and set aside, still damp.

Warm the olive oil in a separate frying or sauté pan and fry the bacon, tossing it from time to time, until it begins to turn golden all over.

Put the wrapped eggs into the burbling water with their plastic tails sticking up above the water, and be ready to take them out after 3–4 minutes.

Add the chard stalks to the bacon for a couple of minutes, turning, then add the garlic, and after another minute, the damp leaves. Sauté, turning the leaves until they collapse and are soft and shiny all over.

Make and butter your toast. Remove the eggs from the pan and unwrap them. Divide the chard and bacon between the pieces of toast and pop the eggs on top. Season and eat immediately.

better beans on toast — Beans on toast, Mediterranean style. They take about five minutes to make and are instantly satisfying. Butter the toast generously; it makes all the difference.

feeds 4

4 tablespoons olive oil
20g unsalted butter
1 tablespoon finely chopped fresh
  rosemary leaves
3 garlic cloves, smashed and pounded
  to a paste with a little salt
2 x 400g tins cannellini beans, drained
  of all but a little of their liquid

2 handfuls of black olives, stoned and
  roughly chopped
4 large slices sourdough bread (or other
  bread that makes crispy-chewy toast)
Butter, for spreading
Extra virgin olive oil, for drizzling
Salt and freshly ground black pepper

Warm the olive oil and the butter with the rosemary in a large pan for a couple of minutes until sizzling, then add the garlic and stir around for another minute or two – you want it to just cook, not burn.

Then add the beans with a little of their liquid and simmer for a few minutes to soften them. Remove from the heat and stir in the olives. Check for seasoning – the olives will probably make it salty enough.

Toast and butter the bread and tip the beans on top, finishing with a generous drizzle of extra virgin olive oil and plenty of fresh black pepper.

three everyday soups

smoky butternut soup — This soup is comfortingly silky and very filling, perfect for an autumn evening when you want something soothing yet still a bit sophisticated. As with all soups, it's worth remembering the better the stock, the better the soup.

feeds 4

50g butter
1 large onion, chopped
1 large butternut squash, peeled, deseeded and roughly chopped
175g smoked streaky bacon or pancetta, roughly chopped

14 good-sized sage leaves
500ml fresh chicken stock, or ½ good stock cube
Salt and freshly ground black pepper
Crusty bread (p.247), to serve

Melt half the butter in a large pan, and sweat the onion, butternut, bacon and two of the sage leaves very gently, lid on, for about 10 minutes, checking every so often that nothing is sticking or burning.

If you are using a stock cube, make it up half strength. Add enough stock to just cover the vegetables. Partly cover and simmer gently for 15–20 minutes until the butternut is completely tender.

Remove from the heat and allow to cool off a little. Blend until smooth. Season to taste (you may not need extra salt due to the bacon) and divide between bowls. Finally, melt the rest of the butter in a small frying pan until foaming and add the rest of the sage leaves. Fry until crispy and starting to turn golden, and use to garnish each bowl of soup. Serve with good, crusty bread.

lentil, pear and rocket soup

— This soup wavers between the substantial and the delicate, with the earthy flavours of lentil and the spiky rocket lifted and subtly sweetened by the pear.

feeds 4

Olive oil, for cooking
1 medium onion, finely chopped
1 carrot, finely chopped
1 stick celery, finely chopped
1 garlic clove, crushed
250g brown lentils

500ml good chicken stock
60g wild rocket
1 pear
Salt and freshly ground black
 pepper
Extra virgin olive oil, to serve

Add a little olive oil to a large pan and sweat the onion, carrot and celery for 5 minutes, so that they begin to soften but not colour. Add the garlic and cook for another 5 minutes.

Add the lentils to the pan and turn to coat in the oil, add the stock, bring to the boil and simmer for 30 minutes until the lentils are tender. Add the rocket to the pan for the last 5 minutes of cooking, then remove from the heat.

Peel, core and chop the pear into small cubes. Transfer two thirds of the soup to the blender, add the pear and whizz to your desired texture – I like to keep it quite chunky. You may need a little water or extra stock to thin it down. Return the whizzed soup to the pan and mix with the remaining soup. Check for seasoning, and serve with a swirl of best oil on top.

spiced carrot soup – There's a punchy heat to this soup which makes it equally delicious as a cleansing evening soup (particularly if you have a cold), or a dramatic, summery lunch or supper, iced the following day.

feeds 4

Groundnut oil, for frying
1 medium onion, roughly chopped
400g carrots, roughly chopped
5cm piece fresh root ginger, peeled and
  finely chopped

1 teaspoon ground coriander
½ teaspoon ground ginger
400ml vegetable stock
100ml coconut milk (optional)
Salt

Add a little oil to a large pan and gently sweat the onion and carrots, with the lid on, for 5 minutes. Add the spices, stir and turn thoroughly, then cover again for 1 minute. Add the stock and simmer for 30 minutes.

Transfer the soup to a blender or processor and blend until smooth. Season to taste. If you prefer a milder soup, add some coconut milk to help counteract the spiciness and warm through again before eating.

three store-cupboard pastas

goodfellas spaghetti pomodoro – My friend Claire learned how to make this from the final scene in *Goodfellas*. It is to my mind one of the truly great tomato sauces for spaghetti, or just a daily treat, however you want to think of it. Covered with a slick of oil it will keep in the fridge for a week or so.

feeds 4

4 tablespoons good olive oil
1 medium red onion
2 garlic cloves, finely chopped
400g tin chopped tomatoes
1 teaspoon caster sugar

400g spaghetti
Knob of butter
Salt and freshly ground black pepper
Fresh basil leaves and grated
   Parmesan, to serve

Warm 1 tablespoon of the olive oil in a heavy-based frying pan. Dice half the onion and slice the other half, then fry gently in the olive oil until soft and translucent – about 5 minutes. Add half the garlic, and stir for a minute, then add the tomatoes, sugar and seasoning. Cook gently, half covered, for 40 minutes – if it looks too dry, top up with water. After 40 minutes, turn off the heat and add the rest of the garlic, stirring to disperse it.

Meanwhile, cook the spaghetti in a big saucepan of well-salted, boiling water until al dente. Add the butter and stir well.

When the sauce has sat with the garlic for 5 minutes, check the seasoning, stir in the remaining oil and toss with the spaghetti. Serve immediately with torn fresh basil and grated Parmesan.

farfalle with broad beans and feta

farfalle with broad beans and feta — This bright and fresh bowl of pasta is all the more pleasing for coming from long-lasting stores. Unless I can pick broad beans off the plant myself, I prefer to use baby frozen ones, which are a great asset to keep in the freezer. Here they are set off by delicate dill, but you can happily replace it with fresh mint for a summery alternative.

feeds 4

400g farfalle
400g frozen or fresh baby broad beans
200g feta cheese
2 tablespoons chopped fresh dill or mint,
  plus a few extra chopped fronds or
  leaves, to serve
5 tablespoons good olive oil
Freshly ground black pepper

Cook the pasta in plenty of well-salted, boiling water according to the packet instructions. Drain, reserving 2 tablespoons of the pasta cooking liquor.

Bring the broad beans just to the boil then drain, and plunge into cold water so that they retain their bright green colour. Slip one third of the beans out of their skins, then set aside. In a food processor, blend the rest with the feta and the dill or mint and olive oil and the reserved cooking liquor. Season with black pepper.

Stir the puréed mixture into the cooked pasta, along with the peeled beans. Scatter with a few fronds of dill or chopped mint leaves. Delicious eaten immediately, or cold as a salad, later.

creamy sausage pasta with peas

— This quick and easy pasta dish is made out of corner-shop staples, making it a reliable friend in any situation. It is as comforting to eat as it is simple to make, and would work well with any type of sausage: fragrant and herby, garlicky or spicy.

feeds 4

600g sausagemeat or 8–10 sausages
  squeezed out of their skins
2 tablespoons olive oil
1 tablespoon finely chopped fresh sage
2 garlic cloves, finely chopped
1 glass dry white wine

500g fusilli
4 large handfuls of frozen peas
150ml double cream
Grated Parmesan and freshly ground
  black pepper, to serve

Fry the sausagemeat in the oil in a sauté pan or flameproof casserole large enough that you can press it out in a fairly thin layer – this will enable it to colour and caramelise rather than steam. Allow it to cook for a few minutes until it really begins to colour before turning and breaking it up.

When it begins to resemble coarse mince and is starting to colour all over, add the sage. Continue frying for a couple of minutes, then add the garlic, turning all the time so the ingredients cook evenly. Add the wine, allow to bubble up then turn down the heat, cover and allow to gently simmer for 10 minutes or so.

Meanwhile, cook the pasta in plenty of well-salted, boiling water. When it is nearly cooked, turn the heat up on the sauce again (the wine should be nearly evaporated), and add the peas. Stir for a minute or two.

Drain the pasta and reserve a little cooking liquor. Add the cream to the sauce and warm it through, then toss through the pasta, adding a little of the pasta cooking liquor if you need to loosen the sauce up. Grate over plenty of fresh Parmesan and black pepper, to serve.

a fishy collection

fish and chips – You need to get your short order chef's hat on for this, or use two large frying pans, so that you can get all the fish cooked at the same time. Otherwise, cook the fish in two batches and keep hot on a plate lined with kitchen paper in a warm oven for a couple of minutes while you cook the second batch.

Traditionally this is accompanied by rustic chips, tartare sauce and puréed peas, but for an Eastern kick I sometimes like to serve with a good dollop of Minted tahini sauce (p.273).

feeds 4

3 tablespoons plain flour
40g butter
1 tablespoon sunflower oil
4 lemon sole fillets
Salt and freshly ground black pepper
Rustic chips (p.272) and lemon wedges,
  to serve

for the tartare sauce:
6 mini cornichons
2 tablespoons capers in brine, drained
4 heaped tablespoons good-quality
  mayonnaise
Good squeeze of lemon juice

Preheat the oven to the lowest setting.

Shake the flour onto a large plate and season very well. Melt half the butter and oil in a large frying pan. Dredge the first two fish fillets in the flour on both sides then fry, skin-side down, till golden and crispy, about 2–3 minutes. Flip over and repeat on the other side. The fish will be cooked when the thickest part in the middle is opaque and lifts easily from the bone. Transfer to the oven to keep warm and repeat with the remaining fish fillets.

To make the tartare sauce, finely chop the cornichons and capers and stir into the mayonnaise, along with a squeeze of lemon juice.

Serve the fish with the tartare sauce, chips and a wedge of lemon – and, if you want to go the whole hog, peas roughly blended with butter and freshly chopped mint.

mackerel niçoise — This can turn itself to any situation, from a simple supper at home, to a summer lunch outside. There are endless different variations of this dish and you can play with whatever ingredients you like, adding an extra something such as broad beans, fresh peas, chickpeas or artichoke hearts, if they take your fancy.

feeds 4

for the salad:
450g small waxy potatoes, eg Jersey Royal or Pink Fir Apple
4 eggs
450g green beans, topped
15 cherry tomatoes, halved
15–20 small black olives

50g tin anchovies in olive oil
3 tablespoons plain flour
Olive oil, for frying
4 mackerel fillets
Salt and freshly ground black pepper

for the dressing:
1 garlic clove
8 tablespoons extra virgin olive oil
Juice of 1 lemon

First add the potatoes (no need to peel) to a large pan of boiling salted water.

Now make the dressing by pounding the garlic with a little salt, then add the oil and lemon juice. Put into a large mixing bowl.

After the potatoes have been cooking for 15 minutes, add the eggs to the pan, and then the beans 2 minutes later. Cook for a further 5 minutes. Plunge the potatoes, eggs and beans into a big bowl of cold water, then drain thoroughly.

Slice the potatoes roughly and add them to the dressing with the beans, tomatoes and olives. Toss carefully but thoroughly. Arrange the dressed ingredients on a large shallow platter. Peel and quarter the eggs and lay around the edge. Drain the anchovies and lay them over the top.

When you are ready to eat, put the flour on a plate and season it. Warm a griddle pan or non-stick frying pan over a high heat with a little olive oil. Make 2 or 3 slashes in the mackerel skin, dredge both sides in flour and add to the pan, skin-side down. Fry for a couple of minutes, then turn down the heat a little and cook on for another minute or two. It's important not to move the fish until the skin has crisped up or it will tear and fall apart. Turn over, fry for another minute, lay over the salad and serve immediately.

spiced pollack with saffron mash — There is a perfect
match in this silky, fragrant potato and the gentle warmth of the spiced fish.
Just a word of warning here – don't season the potatoes with pepper, it will kill
the delicate flavour of the saffron.

feeds 4

½ teaspoon ground turmeric
1 tablespoon ground coriander
1 teaspoon ground ginger
½ teaspoon hot chilli powder
4 tablespoons plain flour
4 x 200g thick-cut pollack fillets or other
  firm white fish fillet
1 tablespoon groundnut or vegetable oil
1 tablespoon butter
Broccoli with olive oil and lemon (p.270)
  and lemon wedges, to serve

for the mash:
600g floury potatoes, eg Maris Piper,
  King Edward or Desiree
120ml whole milk
Generous pinch saffron threads
Knob of butter
Salt

First, start the mash. Boil the potatoes (no need to peel but if they are very
large you may need to chop them first) in lightly salted water, until tender.
Drain and return to the pan. When cool enough to handle, slip off the skins.
Pour the milk into a small pan, add the saffron and bring almost to the boil.
Pour the saffron milk over the potatoes, add the butter and a little salt, if you
like, and mash until smooth. Cover to keep warm.

Meanwhile, preheat the oven to 200°C/gas 6.

To prepare the fish, mix the spices into the flour with a pinch of salt and dredge
the fish on both sides, shaking off any excess. Heat the oil and butter in a frying
pan large enough to take all the fillets and fry for a couple of minutes, skin-side
down, until golden and crispy. Turn and repeat on the other side, then transfer
to the oven for 5 minutes or so, until just cooked and beginning to easily flake.

Serve the fish with lemon wedges, the mash and broccoli.

japanese mackerel — This is savoury but with the pleasingly sweet roundness that is characteristic of so much Japanese food. The fish takes just a few minutes to make, so the rice with which it is served will need to be almost cooked when you start. Oriental roast butternut with seeds (p.271) works well as a side dish.

feeds 4

2 teaspoons sesame oil
4 tablespoons dark soy sauce
4 tablespoons mirin
2 small garlic cloves, finely chopped

3cm piece fresh root ginger, finely chopped
4 mackerel fillets
Brown rice and sliced avocado, to serve

Beat together the sesame oil, soy sauce, mirin, garlic and ginger. Make a couple of slashes in the skin of each fillet and turn them in the mixture. Fry for 2 minutes on each side in a dry non-stick pan over a medium heat until just cooked through.

When nearly ready, add the rest of the sauce to warm through and briefly cook. Serve the mackerel on the brown rice with avocado slices and the rest of the sauce drizzled on top.

moules marinière — It's easy to overlook mussels, and place them in the 'restaurant food' category. In fact, they are one of the simplest things to cook at home. They have the added bonus of being plentiful, home-grown, and readily available. The key is to make sure they are washed of all grit. Serve with crusty pesto bread for added zip.

feeds 4

3kg mussels
2 sprigs flat-leaf parsley, plus
   a handful of parsley leaves,
   roughly chopped
2 sprigs thyme
2 bay leaves

25g butter
2 garlic cloves, finely chopped
3 shallots, finely chopped
1 small glass dry white wine or cider
4 tablespoons double cream
Pesto bread (p.242), to serve

Wash the mussels under plenty of cold, running water. The movement of the water is the important bit – if the water is still the mussels will close up with all the grit inside them. Discard any open mussels that won't close when lightly tapped. Pull out the tough, fibrous beards from between the tightly closed shells and then knock off any barnacles with a large knife. Give the mussels another quick rinse to remove any little pieces of shell.

Tie the herbs together with some string or an elastic band. Melt the butter in a pan big enough to take all the mussels (they should only half fill the pan). Soften the garlic and shallots in the butter with the herbs.

Add the mussels and wine or cider, turn up the heat, then cover and steam the mussels open in their own juices for 3–4 minutes. Give the pan a good shake every now and then.

Remove the herbs, add the cream and chopped parsley and take off the heat. Ladle into four large warmed bowls and serve with pesto bread.

good for kids

pasta with quick tomato sauce

Crush garlic and sizzle for a minute in olive oil. Add passata, a little sugar and salt, and cook for 5 minutes. Toss your cooked pasta with plenty of butter first, and then with the sauce, tearing basil leaves over if you have them (it's perfectly good without). Plenty of Parmesan here, please.

garam masala bashed chicken

Mix 2 teaspoons garam masala with 3 tablespoons plain flour. Chop a skinless chicken breast into four and bash out into thin escalopes. Dredge generously in the flour and fry in a non-stick pan greased with a little groundnut oil, until just turning golden. Eat with rice and tzatziki.

garlic lamb cutlets with houmous

Rub lamb cutlets with olive oil, finely chopped garlic, a little salt and pepper, and pan-fry for 2–3 minutes on each side. Spread on a smear of houmous and serve with toasted pitta bread and Greek salad on the side.

cheese toasties

Be imaginative with the fillings: try blue cheese and pear, smoked ham and fontina, feta and black olive, as well as Cheddar and ham; all work beautifully. Sandwich between two slices of bread, and butter the outside. Heat a non-stick frying pan and place the sandwich inside, pressing down with a metal spatula. When golden underneath, flip over and repeat.

sausage burger

Split lengthways and butterfly best-quality sausages, then pan-fry – you shouldn't need extra fat if you have a non-stick pan – for 5 minutes on each side until golden and juicy. Transfer to a soft, buttered, roll and stuff with red onion rings, lettuce and slices of ripe tomato.

When cooking for children, you take your chances. What they do or don't like at any given moment is as random as a shower on a sunny day. They can declare themselves to be starving and only nibble at a crust, or uninterested then tuck into a full-sized steak. They can loathe spinach for months then clamour for it, or turn off rice when it's the only thing left in the house. Some will happily nibble on anchovies and olives before the age of one, others will not get much beyond buttered pasta for years.

In principle, I don't believe in 'kids' food'. Children should, as soon as they can, take part in family meals, learn to sit still at the table, and take on grown-up textures and flavours. That's the theory, anyway. But in all honesty, as a parent, what you most want is simply to get them safely and happily through the day. As far as food is concerned, that means making sure what they eat is wholesome, nourishing and appealing.

This chapter is packed with recipes for food that, by and large, children love. All recipes are written to feed four adults, partly because it's almost impossible to say what a child's portion should be, and partly in the hope that you'll all be eating together. You will find here the smooth, round flavours and soft textures that few will turn their noses up at, small shapes that are easy to manage for small fingers, dishes to dip into, slurp up and crunch on. There are a few gentle challenges, too, hints of spices and sauces to take them a little further afield, but nothing too demanding. It is lowest-common-denominator eating at its best.

It should also present few challenges for the cook. Children's food should not be demanding to make – not only because it's dispiriting if you've laboured only for it to be refused but also because if you become resentful over it, it introduces a power play. Cook it quickly, and simply, make it delicious, and move on. If it tastes good enough for you to eat, it's good enough for them. If they won't eat it, clear it away and say nothing. How you eat is an important part of growing up, but it's only a part of it.

No drama.

many veg bolognese — This is a wonderfully rich, sweet ragu that pretty much hides its vegetables. It takes a bit of time to make but it's a great family staple to have in the freezer. Eat either with pasta or mash.

feeds 4 adults

2 onions
2 sticks celery
2 large or 4 medium carrots
1 medium parsnip
½ butternut squash
¼ cauliflower
Olive oil, for frying
4 garlic cloves, peeled and bashed
600g beef mince

100ml whole milk
400g tin chopped tomatoes
2 sprigs thyme
200ml chicken stock, red wine, white wine or water
Worcestershire sauce, to taste
2 tablespoons tomato ketchup
Pasta or mash and grated Cheddar cheese, to serve

Roughly chop all the fresh vegetables and then put them into a food processor to pulse into fairly small pieces. There will be a few larger chunks left which won't matter unless you have carrot-averse children.

Pour 4 tablespoons of olive oil into a large flameproof casserole and fry the vegetables over a high heat until they are sizzling. Before they begin to colour, lower the heat and cook gently, stirring from time to time for 20 minutes until soft and golden. Add the garlic for the last 5 minutes of cooking.

Preheat the oven to 160°C/gas 3.

Meanwhile, in a non-stick frying pan over a high heat, brown the meat in batches in a couple of tablespoons of olive oil, breaking it up as you go, until it turns golden with crispy bits. Now add the milk. Bring to a bubble and scrape up all the caramelised bits, allowing the milk to nearly evaporate, then transfer the meat, scrapings and juices to the vegetable pan. Add the rest of the ingredients, bring just to a boil, cover and transfer to the oven. Cook for 1½–2 hours, checking the liquid every so often and topping up with water if necessary.

Set aside to cool a little, then skim the surface of excess fat and remove the thyme stalks. Serve with pasta or mash and plenty of grated cheese.

special fried rice – This dish is packed with interesting flavours, and appealingly small pieces, and more often than not you will have most of the ingredients in the kitchen. It is particularly useful in that the number of ingredients can happily expand or contract depending on what you have available. It's an excellent way of using up leftovers, and almost anything can go in. In our house, it most regularly consists of just rice, eggs, peas and nuts.

feeds 4 adults

240g white or basmati rice
4 tablespoons sesame oil
2 eggs
2.5cm piece fresh root ginger, peeled and finely chopped
4 garlic cloves, finely chopped
4 heaped tablespoons finely chopped leftover cooked chicken or pork (optional)

4 heaped tablespoons frozen peeled North Atlantic prawns (optional)
3 tablespoons raw or roasted peanuts or cashews, roughly crushed
1 large handful of frozen petits pois
160g tin sweetcorn, drained
Light soy sauce, to serve

First, cook the rice: rinse it in cold water, and put it in a saucepan with enough cold water to cover it by 1.5cm. Cover, bring to the boil, reduce to a simmer and cook for 10–12 minutes until the water is absorbed and the rice al dente. Remove from the heat, take off the lid and allow to sit for a couple of minutes, then fluff with a fork.

Meanwhile, heat 2 tablespoons of the oil until smoking in a wok or large non-stick frying pan. Break in the eggs. Stir furiously so that they break up. When the egg is dry and well cooked, push it over to the side of the pan. Add ½ tablespoon of the oil and the remaining ingredients apart from the rice, and stir until cooked through.

Finally, add the rest of the oil and the rice, stirring everything together until coated and hot. Divide between plates and sprinkle over a few drops of soy sauce to serve.

cornflake fish fingers — These golden fingers are all the brighter and crisper here for their coating of cornflakes. The Parmesan should replace the need for salt.

feeds 4 adults

600g pollack or haddock fillet,
   skinned
2 tablespoons finely grated
   Parmesan cheese
2 tablespoons plain flour
2 eggs, beaten

70g crushed cornflakes
Vegetable or sunflower oil, for frying
Peas and Rustic chips (p.272), or
   buttered bread and tomato ketchup,
   to serve

Preheat the oven to 110°C/gas ¼.

Cut the fish into strips about 5 x 2cm. Mix the Parmesan with the flour and turn the fish in it. Dip into the beaten egg, and then turn in the cornflakes till coated.

Heat a few tablespoons of oil in a non-stick frying pan over a medium heat. Fry the fish fingers, in batches if necessary, until golden on all sides, about 5 minutes altogether, making sure not to pack the pan too tightly.

Keep extra cooked fish fingers warm in the oven on a plate with some foil over them if you are doing them in batches.

Serve with peas and rustic chips or in buttered bread, and some ketchup on the side.

chicken pasta soup

chicken pasta soup — This simple chicken broth is a great warmer, as well as being easy to eat and very nourishing. Small children might find it easier to eat the 'bits' from a bowl and drink the broth from a cup.

feeds 4 adults

4 chicken drumsticks
4 chicken wings
2 large carrots, chopped
2 onions, quartered
1 stick celery, chopped

1 bay leaf
100g stelline or other pasta shapes
Lemon, for squeezing, and soy sauce,
  to serve (optional)

Put all the ingredients except the pasta into a large pan and cover with water by 2cm. Bring gently to the boil, skimming off any scum that rises to the surface. Reduce to a gentle simmer, partially cover, and simmer for 1–2 hours, topping up with a little water every so often.

Remove from the heat, pour into a bowl and set aside to allow it to cool long enough for the fat to pool on the surface, then skim most of it off.

Strain the liquid through a sieve, back into the pan. Pick out the chicken, and discard the bones and skin, setting aside the strips of meat and the carrots and celery. Remove the onions and bay leaf, and discard.

Add the pasta to the soup, bring back to the boil and simmer for 7 minutes (or the time specified on the pasta's packet instructions), adding a little extra water if the pot seems low on liquid.

Return the meat and vegetables to the pan and divide the soup between bowls or mugs. Serve with a squeeze of lemon juice or a dash of soy sauce, if desired.

sticky garlic drumsticks

sticky garlic drumsticks — This is more scented than overwhelmed by garlic, despite the volume used. It's a great way to introduce garlic without making it into a drama. More adventurous children will like to peel off the papery skins and squeeze out the sweet garlic to eat alongside.

feeds 4 adults

2 tablespoons plain flour
2 teaspoons smoked sweet paprika
8 chicken drumsticks
5 tablespoons olive oil
1 whole garlic head, cloves separated
  but unpeeled

Salt and freshly ground black pepper
Rice and steamed green vegetables,
  to serve

Place the flour, paprika and some seasoning in a large plastic food bag and add the drumsticks. Give the bag a good shake to evenly coat the chicken.

Heat the olive oil in a large frying pan and add the drumsticks and garlic cloves. Fry, turning, until they start to become golden, then sprinkle over 2 tablespoons water. Cover, with the lid ajar, and cook for a further 20–25 minutes, turning every so often. The liquid should have reduced to leave a sticky, garlicky, coating.

Serve the drumsticks with the soft, sweet garlic and the rice and veg alongside.

monika's prawn and courgette couscous – This ten-minute supper from corner-shop ingredients results in a steaming, fragrant bowl of couscous. You could replace the prawns with any cooked protein: cubed tofu, or even simply a couple of handfuls of pumpkin seeds.

feeds 4 adults

375g frozen North Atlantic prawns
2 handfuls of frozen petits pois
¼ chicken stock cube
3 tablespoons olive oil
2 garlic cloves, very finely chopped

1 tablespoon finely grated fresh ginger
3 carrots, peeled and grated
3 courgettes, grated
½ teaspoon ground cumin
375g couscous

Allow the prawns and peas to defrost, then drain off any liquid. Dissolve the ¼ chicken stock cube in 600ml boiling water.

Heat the oil in a saucepan over a medium-high heat, and fry the garlic and ginger for a minute. Add the carrots, courgettes and cumin, and fry together for 5 minutes, until just softening but not coloured.

Add the prawns, peas and couscous and pour over the boiling stock. Cover, simmer for a minute, then remove from the heat and allow the rest of the liquid to be absorbed for 5 minutes. Fluff with a fork, and divide between bowls.

rustic chorizo tortilla — This is an excellent way of feeding

a number of kids or 4 adults. It is delicious warm and even better cold, the following day.

feeds 4 adults
you will need a 20cm frying pan

6 tablespoons olive oil
1 large Spanish onion, roughly
  chopped
150g mild chorizo sausage
500g new potatoes

500ml sunflower oil
6 eggs
2 tablespoons chopped flat-leaf
  parsley (optional)
Salt and freshly ground black pepper

First heat the olive oil in the frying pan and cook the onion gently until it turns golden and sweet – this will take about half an hour, which gives you enough time to get everything else done.

Squeeze the chorizo out of its skin and chop into small pieces. Add to the onion after 15 minutes, remembering to stir and turn from time to time.

Slice the potatoes into 5mm-thick discs (no need to peel). Warm the sunflower oil to about 170°C in a large saucepan (it should not be more than half full), and gently fry the potatoes until they are fairly soft but not coloured; this will take about 15 minutes. Remove the potatoes using a slotted spoon and place on kitchen paper. You can keep the oil to use again.

When the onion and chorizo are ready, remove them from the pan with a slotted spoon and place on a plate lined with kitchen paper, reserving the oil.

Beat the eggs in a large mixing bowl or jug, and add the onion, chorizo, potatoes and parsley, season with confidence and stir carefully to combine without breaking up the potatoes.

Heat a couple of tablespoons of the onion oil in the frying pan until smoking hot. Tip the egg mixture in, turn the heat down and cook it until the bottom firms up and turns golden (about 5–6 minutes). Invert a dinner plate over the pan and with one smooth movement turn the tortilla over so that the cooked half is on the top. Slide it back into the pan to cook the other side. It should be ready in another 3–5 minutes.

houmous plate

israeli houmous — Like the Israelis I prefer my houmous silky smooth, so I make it in a blender rather than a processor. I rarely find tinned chickpeas are soft enough to make smooth houmous, but don't often have the inclination to soak and cook my own. Instead I cook tinned ones a little longer, and it seems to do the trick. However, if you can find the very large, soft, Spanish chickpeas that come in glass bottles they are just perfect, and won't need the extra cooking.

These dips will all last for 4 or 5 days in sealed containers in the fridge, and are great as adults' snacks – just add an extra swirl of extra virgin olive oil and a good pinch of sea salt.

feeds 4 adults

300g tinned, drained chickpeas
½ teaspoon bicarbonate of soda
2 fat garlic cloves

125g tahini
4 tablespoons lemon juice
Salt

Empty the chickpeas into a saucepan, with the bicarbonate of soda, and top up with water to cover by 3cm or so. Cover, bring to the boil and cook for 20 minutes until totally soft and easy to mush. Drain, reserving the cooking liquid.

Crush the garlic with a pinch of salt to form a paste.

Blend all the ingredients together, until smooth, using the cooking water to loosen it until it's a soft consistency that only just holds its shape.

beetroot houmous — The rich and sweet flavours of this regally hued houmous would also work well alongside lamb and fish.

feeds 4 adults

1 large or 2 medium beetroot (about 200g)
1 garlic clove
4 tablespoons tahini
2 tablespoons Greek yoghurt
4 tablespoons olive oil
Splash of red wine vinegar
Salt

Boil the beetroot until tender, about 30–40 minutes. Once cooked and cool enough to handle, peel and roughly chop.

Crush the garlic with a pinch of salt to form a paste. Blend all the ingredients together until smooth and season with salt, to taste.

pumpkin houmous — This houmous is sweet and creamy. It's also excellent alongside lamb for a grown-up supper.

feeds 4 adults

½ small pumpkin, peeled, deseeded and cut into chunks (about 300g)
1 small garlic clove
Pinch ground cumin
3 tablespoons olive oil
3 tablespoons tahini
Lemon juice, to taste
Salt

Steam the pumpkin chunks for 10 minutes until they are tender. Set aside to dry out.

Crush the garlic with a little salt and the cumin to form a paste.

Put the pumpkin in a blender with the garlic mixture, olive oil and tahini and pulse until nearly smooth. Add lemon juice and salt to taste and pulse again. Serve warm with rack of lamb for a posh, interesting dinner or at room temperature as a dip.

a versatile roast vegetable sauce for pasta or pizza

My friend Lucinda always has a version of this sauce in the fridge – it's extremely handy if you want to knock up a quick bowl of pasta or pizza for hungry kids. It will keep for a week, with a thin slick of olive oil over the top.

feeds 4 adults

2 medium onions, topped, tailed, peeled and cut into wedges
2 large carrots, chopped into 1.5cm pieces
2 sweet peppers, quartered and deseeded
½ medium butternut squash, peeled, deseeded and chopped into 1.5cm cubes

Olive oil
1 garlic clove, finely chopped or pounded
200ml passata
1 sprig basil (optional)
Salt (optional)

Preheat the oven to 200°C/gas 6.

Put the onions, carrots, peppers and squash into a large roasting tin, drizzle with olive oil and sprinkle with salt if you are using it, turning with your hands until well coated. Roast for 25 minutes, then turn, covering with foil if they are starting to catch and burn in places. Cook for a further 15 minutes until soft and sweet.

Meanwhile, heat a little olive oil in a small pan, fry the garlic for a couple of minutes then add the passata and simmer for 5 minutes. Remove from the heat.

When all the vegetables are cooked, discard any burnt bits and mix together with the passata. Tear in the basil and blend the sauce in a food processor, in batches if necessary, until it is as smooth as you can make it.

For almost instant pizza, spread over tortillas or halved pitta breads, sprinkle generously with grated mozzarella and top with whatever else you like (eg ham, sliced mushrooms), then bake in the oven at 230°C/gas 8 for 5 minutes.

tomato risotto — This is a store-cupboard risotto that is hard to fault – smooth, soothing and sustaining. You could add some bacon or chorizo at the start for something a little meatier, and/or some torn basil at the end, if you have some to hand.

feeds 4 adults

40g butter
3 tablespoons olive oil
1 onion, finely chopped
240g risotto rice
200ml passata
1 litre hot chicken stock

A few torn basil leaves (optional)
Large handful of grated Parmesan
  cheese
Sea salt and freshly ground black
  pepper

Heat the butter and 1 tablespoon of the olive oil in a large pan. Gently fry the onion until soft and translucent but not coloured.

Add the rice and stir around for a minute until thoroughly coated in the butter and oil. Add the passata and a ladleful of hot stock, and bring to a simmer, stirring constantly. Keep adding the stock, ladle by ladle, as the rice absorbs it, stirring all the while. It should take 15–20 minutes or so until completely cooked – the rice should be soft but still retain a little bite, and have a creamy, dropping consistency. Season to taste.

Drizzle the remaining olive oil over the top of the risotto, garnish with the basil, if using, and serve with the grated Parmesan.

arancini — These balls of baked or fried risotto are a delicious way of using up any leftovers and work well in lunchboxes and for picnics, too. You can hide anything in the middle – a cube of ham, strips of prosciutto, or simply stick with mozzarella.

makes 12 balls

6 heaped tablespoons breadcrumbs or polenta

12 tablespoons tomato risotto (opposite), cooled and chilled, or any leftover risotto

1 large egg, lightly beaten

12 small cubes mozzarella

Olive oil, for cooking

Steamed broccoli or crudités, to serve

Spread out the breadcrumbs or polenta on a plate.

Mix the risotto and egg to form a sticky paste. With damp hands, form the rice into 12 balls, pushing a cube of mozzarella, and whatever else you'd like to include, into the centre.

Close up the hole and roll the balls in the breadcrumbs or polenta until coated all over. Set aside in the fridge for 30 minutes.

To oven bake, preheat the oven to 200°C/gas 6. Arrange the balls on a lightly oiled baking tray and brush generously with oil. Bake for 20 minutes, turning, until golden brown.

To fry, heat about 5mm of oil in a frying pan and fry in batches, until evenly golden and perfectly crisp. Transfer to drain on kitchen paper and serve hot with steamed broccoli. Or allow to cool, then chill and serve with crudités.

chicken and broccoli teriyaki —

This is a Japanese childhood favourite; its sweet stickiness will tempt the fussiest of eaters. It has a certain amount of salt and sugar in it, which is reduced here by using a low-salt variety of soy sauce, and a natural sugar such as agave nectar or honey. Serve with white rice. This is a good dish to introduce chopsticks.

feeds 4 adults

4 skinless, boneless chicken breasts
   or 6 skinless, boneless thighs, chopped
   into bite-sized pieces
4 tablespoons cornflour
2 tablespoons vegetable oil
300g small broccoli florets
White rice, to serve

for the sauce:
7 tablespoons reduced-salt soy sauce
8 tablespoons mirin
4 tablespoons agave nectar or clear honey

First, make the teriyaki sauce by combining the soy sauce, mirin and agave nectar or honey in a jug.

Put the chopped chicken in a large plastic food bag with the cornflour. Give it a good shake to evenly coat the chicken.

Heat the oil in a non-stick frying pan and fry the chicken until it is brown all over.

Meanwhile, boil or steam the broccoli florets for 3–4 minutes until they are just al dente.

Pour the teriyaki sauce over the chicken in the pan and allow it to bubble for a couple of minutes until slightly thickened and the chicken is cooked through. Add the broccoli after a minute.

Serve with white rice.

not-too-chilli con carne — Chilli has somehow gone out of fashion, which is a shame when it's brilliant for feeding a multigenerational crowd. Each can make of it what they will – rolling the whole spread into tortillas makes a great burrito. To make it more fiery, add 2 finely chopped red chillies to the onions at the start and/or a splash or two of Tabasco sauce.

feeds 4 adults

2 medium onions, peeled
2 garlic cloves, peeled
1 carrot, peeled
1 stick celery
2 red peppers, halved and deseeded
Olive oil, for frying
1 teaspoon ground cumin
1 teaspoon ground cinnamon
1 teaspoon smoked sweet or hot paprika
200g fresh chorizo sausages
500g beef mince
500ml passata

400g tin kidney beans, drained
400g tin cannellini beans, drained
2 small squares 85% cocoa solids dark
   chocolate

serving suggestions:
Avocados mashed with lime juice
   and olive oil
Greek yoghurt
White rice
Grated Cheddar cheese
Tortillas
Chopped fresh coriander

Preheat the oven to 180°C/gas 4.

Finely chop or whizz the onions, garlic, carrot, celery and peppers. Add a couple of glugs of olive oil to a large flameproof casserole, and soften the vegetables over a medium heat for about 10 minutes, adding the spices for the last minute.

Remove the skins from the chorizo, break them up and brown, along with the mince, in a large, non-stick frying pan. Once golden, add the meat to the casserole.

Measure out 200ml water and deglaze the meat pan with a little of the water to loosen the caramelised bits. Transfer the meat juices to the casserole.

Add the passata, the remaining water and the beans to the casserole. Bring just to the boil, cover and transfer to the oven for 1½ hours. Check the liquid level occasionally and add more water if it looks too dry.

When the meat is cooked through, tender and fragrant, stir in the chocolate. Serve the chilli with your choice of the serving suggestions.

treats for two

treats for two ... in a rush

spaghetti with crab, chilli and parsley

Mix white and brown crab meat together, adding plenty of lemon juice, olive oil, some finely chopped fresh red chilli (seeds discarded) and flat-leaf parsley. Cook pasta until al dente, reserving a spoon or two of the cooking liquor to add to the crab mixture to loosen it up a little. Toss all together, and eat immediately, with salt and pepper.

butternut and gorgonzola on toast

Pile roast butternut squash on top of toast and dot Gorgonzola cheese on top of that. Blast under the grill until melted, golden and bubbling.

prawns with feta and chilli

Fry chopped garlic and red chilli in olive oil for a couple of minutes, and add cooked North Atlantic prawns. Toss well, sprinkle feta over, cover and cook for another minute or so, squeeze over lemon, and serve with rice and a green salad.

ripe tomato and serrano ham on toast

Rub toasted sourdough or ciabatta with a garlic clove and drizzle over good olive oil. Rub with the flesh of halved, ripe tomatoes, discarding the skins. Drape over a slice of ham.

flattened spicy sausages with fennel

Squeeze spicy sausages (look for 'Italian' or 'French country' varieties) out of their skins and flatten into a non-stick frying pan. Fry in a scant amount of olive oil for 5 minutes on each side and serve on a bed of very finely sliced fennel bulb.

little gem, halloumi and fig salad

Chop Little Gem lettuce and cucumber into small, 1cm-ish pieces. Cube halloumi to the same size and fry it in a hot pan in olive oil, turning until golden and soft. Add chopped figs for a couple of minutes, turning to warm and soften, and toss with the salad, dressing with olive oil and lemon juice, and a sprinkling of chopped mint and sumac if you have some.

Supper for two is often just a sustaining background to whatever else you may be doing – talking, watching television, sorting out paperwork. But there could, and perhaps should, be a sense of occasion about eating together. This does not always mean a tête-à-tête with your partner. Depending on the rhythms and demands of life, the nature of these duets will change: it may be a heart-to-heart with a girlfriend, a catch-up with a sibling or an early bite with a daughter. More often than not, it will be the moment when you and your partner's days collide before night falls.

Sharing a meal is a way of making that rushed conversation at the end of the day something a little longer and deeper, the moment to delve into an issue that's been nagging away, or simply to toast all being well. This, in other words, is food that has something to say.

This chapter addresses those times when you might have headed out to a restaurant, but life tripped you up – or perhaps the kitchen seemed a cosier place to nourish the soul. It's the sort of food that is a little fancy – not twiddly cooking, just top-notch ingredients, the sort of things you might not buy on an everyday basis. This is where you'll find a juicy steak with onions melting on top, or a whole baked fish sealed with aromatic herbs. While you'll be laying out a bit more up front, the good news is that cost and effort involved are inversely proportional: this is food to bat your eyelashes at, rather than labour intensively over.

Take two minutes extra to complete the picture: lay the table with a cloth, light the candles, dim the lights.

Now you're really saying something.

parma ham with elderflower poached rhubarb and burrata

— This makes a wonderful starter or light lunch, or you can serve it as part of a help-yourself spread. Burrata is buffalo mozzarella's even richer, creamier cousin. It is not widely available, so grab it from an Italian deli whenever you see it. Buffalo mozzarella would work beautifully, too.

Any remaining poaching liquid makes a delicious treat to serve for breakfast with Greek yoghurt and muesli, or drizzled over vanilla ice cream.

feeds 2

200g rhubarb
250ml elderflower cordial
3 tablespoons sugar (optional)
8 slices Parma ham
2 balls burrata or buffalo mozzarella
   cheese

2 heads fresh elderflower or 4 sprigs mint
Freshly ground black pepper
Crusty bread (p.247), to serve

Top and tail the rhubarb and chop into 5cm lengths. In a saucepan, heat all the cordial apart from 3 tablespoons until just starting to boil, adding sugar if the rhubarb is green and tart. Add the rhubarb, cover and poach until it is just tender but still holds its shape, about 5 minutes. Remove with a slotted spoon and set aside to cool, reserving the liquid (see introduction).

When cool, turn the rhubarb in the remaining 3 tablespoons of cordial. Place the rhubarb, Parma ham and burrata or mozzarella on serving plates, and grind over some black pepper. Serve with the elderflower blossom or some chopped mint scattered over the top, along with crusty bread.

baked vacherin with truffled almond crust

— This is a favourite wintry treat – it's basically a fancy fondue, particularly useful around Christmas when you want maximum reward for minimum effort and don't care about the calories. You could easily scale it up for a party by making it with a large cheese – or several – instead.

Whole truffles are famously expensive – if you ever come across truffle salsa, which is a paste made of chopped truffles mixed with good, chopped mushrooms – this is the place to use it. Otherwise, the strength of this cheese can take on truffle oil, which alone can be overpowering.

feeds 2

1 whole small Vacherin Mont d'Or cheese
1 tablespoon truffle salsa or a few drops
   truffle oil
2 tablespoons flaked almonds
Truffle oil, to drizzle

serving suggestions:
Crusty bread (p.247)
Cocktail salami
Cornichons
Mini pickled onions

Preheat the oven to 180°C/gas 4.

Carefully remove the top of the cheese rind to expose the strong creamy cheese inside. Spread the truffle salsa or scatter your truffle oil over the top, followed by a good covering of flaked almonds. Sprinkle over a few drops of truffle oil and bake in the oven for 15 minutes until the cheese is runny and the almonds begin to colour.

Serve the Vacherin with good, crusty bread, cocktail salami, cornichons and mini pickled onions.

pigeon breasts with butternut, pear and pumpkin seed salad

— This warm salad is a perfect autumnal dish – at the same time savoury, sweet, delicate and satisfying.

feeds 2

½ small butternut squash, peeled, deseeded and cut into 1.5cm chunks
Good olive oil
1 fairly ripe pear, peeled, quartered and cored
4 wood pigeon breasts

2 tablespoons dark or tamari soy sauce
1 garlic clove, crushed
1 heaped tablespoon pumpkin seeds
100g wild rocket
½ tablespoon white wine vinegar
Sea salt and freshly ground black pepper

Preheat the oven to 180°C/gas 4.

In a roasting pan, toss the butternut chunks in a tablespoon of oil and sprinkle with sea salt. Roast in the oven for about 40 minutes. Add the pear quarters after about 10 minutes of the roasting time, turning in the oil (you may need a little extra).

Meanwhile, marinate the pigeon breasts for half an hour or so in a tablespoon of olive oil and the same of soy sauce, with half the crushed garlic.

When the butternut and pear are soft and golden remove from the oven and allow to cool for a few minutes. Wipe out the pan and lightly toast the pumpkin seeds on both sides until puffed up and popping.

Pan-fry or griddle the pigeon breasts in a very hot pan over a high heat for 2–3 minutes on each side. Set aside to rest.

In a bowl, add the butternut and pear to the rocket. Dress with the vinegar and 2 tablespoons of olive oil, and the rest of the soy sauce and garlic. Toss gently, then divide between two plates.

Cut the pigeon breasts into slices (they should still be pink in the middle), scatter with pumpkin seeds, salt and pepper, and serve.

penne with roquefort, pink endive and walnuts

This is fabulously rich and tastes deeply luxurious. In small portions, it also makes an excellent starter for a fancy supper.

feeds 2

2 pink endives
Olive oil, for frying
75g shelled walnuts, the fresher the better
100g Roquefort cheese
1 garlic clove, chopped

200g penne
Salt and freshly ground black pepper
Small handful of grated Parmesan cheese, to serve (optional)

Trim the base of the endives and set aside the top third (the tips) of each. Chop the rest into 1cm rounds. Heat a little olive oil in a frying pan and wilt the rounds of endive until just soft and beginning to colour, then set aside.

Grind the walnuts in a processor, then add the Roquefort and garlic, and whizz until you have a rough paste. Transfer to a small bowl.

Cook the penne in plenty of well-salted, boiling water according to the packet instructions. When it is just al dente, drain, reserving some of the cooking liquor. Add a couple of tablespoons of the cooking liquor to loosen the nut and cheese paste. Toss the nut and cheese mixture well through the pasta, adding the raw and cooked endive. Finish with plenty of salt and pepper, and Parmesan if you wish.

lobster and tomato confit spaghetti — This is my favourite
way of eating lobster. It's a real holiday treat when you're by the sea, or a good
way of conjuring up a bit of seaside joy if you can't quite get there.

feeds 2

1 whole live lobster

2 litres seawater or water well salted
   with sea salt

4 large, ripe tomatoes

2 juicy garlic cloves

6 tablespoons extra virgin olive oil

200g spaghetti

Sea salt and freshly ground black pepper

Put the lobster in the freezer for 30 minutes before you want to cook it.

Bring the water to a rolling boil in a pan large enough to fit the lobster. When
the lobster is cold and sleepy, plunge it in. Boil vigorously for 8–10 minutes,
then remove and set aside, straining and reserving the cooking water.

Peel the tomatoes by making a few nicks in them. Place them in a bowl, and
cover with boiling water. Allow to sit for a minute, then slip off the skins. Chop
the tomato flesh, discarding the seeds and the tougher inside membrane. Slice
the garlic very finely.

Warm the olive oil in a small saucepan and add the tomato and garlic. Heat
until just starting to bubble, and cook for 15 minutes until soft and sweet – you
want to turn it into a delicate confit rather than a fried sauce, so be gentle.
Season with salt and pepper.

Bring the lobster water back to the boil in a pan and add the spaghetti.

To remove the meat from the lobster, slice it lengthways, pull out the tail flesh
and break off the claws and legs. Chop up the tail flesh, and when the pasta
is just al dente, drain it and toss with the lobster pieces and oily tomatoes.
Serve the claws and legs over the top, with implements to get into them.

miso pollack – Miso paste is made from fermented soya beans and is diluted with water to make miso soup, the salty, fragrant Japanese broth that is served at the beginning of most meals. There are many different varieties of miso and it is most easily bought from a good health-food shop or online from a Japanese deli (see Directory on p.278 for details).

Here it is used to make a simplified, deliciously silky version of the Japanese restaurant Nobu's black cod. You really do need 24 hours to marinate the fish to get the flavours to come through.

feeds 2

2 x 250g thick cut pollack fillets
500g sweet white miso paste
1 tablespoon groundnut oil

White rice, pickled ginger and steamed green veg with soy sauce and mirin, to serve

Place the pollack in a non-reactive dish, slather completely with the miso paste, cover and marinate in the fridge for 24 hours.

When you are ready to cook, preheat the oven to 200°C/gas 6.

Wipe the miso paste off the fish but do not rinse it off. Heat a few drops of groundnut oil in a sauté pan with an ovenproof handle until medium hot and carefully pan-fry the fillet until turning golden underneath, about 5 minutes. Flip the fillets over, then transfer the pan to the oven and bake for a further 5–10 minutes, depending on the thickness of the fillets. The fish is cooked when it turns opaque and a fork slides easily into the flesh.

Serve with white rice and pickled ginger, as well as steamed spinach, bok choi or broccoli, dressed with soy sauce and a dash of mirin.

salt and pepper quail with rose petal sauce — Unlike

most birds, free-range quail are fatter and juicier than the farmed ones, and really worth visiting a butcher for. I like to spatchcock them so they are flattened and splayed out – it makes it much easier to get at the flesh.

To fill up on them, you want to allow for two to three each, depending on their size. Serve with salad and smooth mash, or take it east, with rice with a dash of soy and mirin.

feeds 2

5–6 free-range quail
Olive oil
Sea salt and freshly ground
    black pepper
Good old green salad (p.271)
    and Smooth mash (p.272), or
    rice with a dash of soy sauce
    and mirin, to serve

for the rose petal sauce:
3 tablespoons rose petal jam,
    or redcurrant jelly
Splash of rosewater
Splash of sherry vinegar
1 garlic clove, crushed
1cm piece fresh root ginger,
    peeled and very finely grated

Preheat the oven to 220°C/gas 7.

To spatchcock quail, place on its breast with the tail nearest to you. With poultry shears or very sharp kitchen scissors, cut down both sides of the backbone and remove it completely. Splay the bird out, giving it a thump with your fist so that it stays flat. Clean the underside carefully. Repeat with the remaining birds. Rub with a little oil and be very generous with the salt and pepper.

Place the birds in roasting trays and cook for 12–15 minutes, turning over half way through. The outside should be golden, the skin crispy, and the leg should come away easily at the joint when you give it a tug.

To make the rose petal sauce, stir all the ingredients together. Serve the quail with the sauce in little bowls for dipping, with salad and mash or rice.

vitello limone — Veal with lemon was always a great childhood treat at a local Italian restaurant. Now that such good rose veal is available from English farms, I have taken to it again with some gusto.

feeds 2

3 tablespoons plain flour
2 x 125g veal scallopines or topside steaks
50g butter
1 teaspoon vegetable oil
1 lemon, for squeezing

2 tablespoons very finely chopped
  flat-leaf parsley
Salt and freshly ground black pepper
Smooth mash (p.272) or Creamed
  spinach (p.270), to serve

Spread the flour on a plate and season with salt and pepper. Dredge the meat on both sides in the flour, shaking off any excess.

Place half the butter and the oil in a large non-stick frying pan over a high heat. When the butter has stopped foaming season it well with black pepper, slip the meat into the pan and cook for just 1 minute on each side. Set aside on a warmed plate.

Reduce the heat under the pan to medium, then squeeze the lemon juice into the pan and scrape off any caramelised residue. Now add the rest of the butter and the parsley to the pan. Once melted, return the meat to the pan, long enough just to warm it through. Serve immediately with mash or creamed spinach.

paddy's pork tenderloin with fennel — My friend Paddy is
an excellent cook and entertains with an insouciance to envy. This is his simple,
yet elegant solution to most situations.

feeds 2

1 x 400g pork tenderloin
1 tablespoon fennel seeds, lightly
  pounded
Olive oil, for frying
1 large fennel bulb, trimmed and cut
  lengthways into 5mm-thick slices

8 small waxy potatoes, halved lengthways
1 small glass white wine
250ml fresh chicken or veal stock
1 tablespoon butter
Salt and freshly ground black pepper
Crusty bread (p.247), to serve

Preheat the oven to 180°C/gas 4.

Roll the pork in the pounded fennel seeds and season. Heat a little olive
oil in a large non-stick frying pan and brown the coated pork. Transfer to
a flameproof casserole.

Gently fry the sliced fennel and the potatoes in the frying pan until they are
beginning to soften and turn golden. Add to the meat, along with the wine
and stock. Bring to the boil and transfer to the oven to cook for 20–25 minutes
depending on the thickness of the meat. Remove the fillet, cover with foil and
set aside to rest.

Add the butter to the fennel and potatoes and reduce on a low heat until you
have a well-flavoured sauce and the fennel is tender. Season to taste, adding
a drop more white wine if necessary.

Slice the fillet diagonally into 2.5cm slices. Spoon the fennel, potatoes and sauce
over the meat, and eat with bread to mop up the juices.

long-marinated rack of lamb tikka – This takes time

for the marinade to really work – a minimum of a day, but two is better. The point is that the enzymes in the yoghurt attack the meat and it becomes unbelievably tender.

The cooking time will depend on how well trimmed the lamb is – supermarkets tend to trim more than butchers.

feeds 2

1 rack of lamb, French trimmed
Juice of ½ lemon
Handful of chopped fresh mint leaves
1 teaspoon turmeric
Pinch chilli powder
½ teaspoon ground coriander
¼ teaspoon ground ginger

½ teaspoon garam masala
450g live natural yoghurt
Salt and freshly ground black pepper
Sautéed potatoes (p.272) sprinkled with
    turmeric and chilli, and Raita (p.191)
    or tzatziki, to serve

Put the lamb in a non-metallic dish or large plastic food bag. Mix the lemon juice, mint and spices into the yoghurt and pour all over the lamb so that it is completely bathed. Seal, wrap or cover and leave in the fridge to marinate for as long as possible, preferably 48 hours.

When you are ready to cook the lamb, preheat the oven to 220°C/gas 7.

Wipe off most of the marinade and transfer the lamb to a roasting tin. Season it with salt and pepper and roast for 25–30 minutes. Allow to rest for 10 minutes before serving.

If the lamb is well trimmed, it looks quite elegant simply cut in half so that you have two steaks of meat, rather than cutlets. Eat with sautéed potatoes with a pinch of turmeric and chilli, and raita or ready-made tzatziki.

steak with blackened spring onions — At home, steak is not something to cook for more than two. However, it is a great treat, and a simple one, too.

You can cook leeks instead of spring onions using this method. Choose young, slim ones, or for fatter ones strip off the outer leaves first.

feeds 2

10 fat spring onions (sometimes labelled 'continental' onions)
2 x 300g sirloin steaks, about 2cm thick, at room temperature

Olive oil, for brushing
Salt and freshly ground black pepper
Perfect baked potatoes (p.272) and English mustard, to serve

To prepare the onions, trim the end off the green stalks and shave off any roots. If they are more than 1.5cm in diameter, halve lengthways. Blanch in boiling, salted water for 1 minute, then drain and allow the moisture to steam off.

Brush the steaks with a little olive oil. Heat a griddle pan until it is smoking, then cook the steaks for 2–3 minutes, until they have begun to develop coloured lines and are no longer sticking to the pan.

Flip them over, and season the first side generously with salt and pepper. When you can see the blood beginning to rise up under the surface of the meat after another 3–4 or so minutes, flip them again, now seasoning the other side. Reduce the heat, and cook for another minute for rare, couple of minutes for medium rare and 3–4 minutes for medium. Remove from the pan and set aside to rest.

Meanwhile, brush a non-stick frying pan with a little olive oil and fry the onions on both sides until the outer layers are blackened and the inside is soft and sweet.

Serve the steaks with the onions alongside, and piping-hot baked potatoes with lots of melting butter, and English mustard for the meat.

comfort cooking

comfort cooking ... in a rush

mushroom stroganoff

Fry a couple of handfuls of wild mushrooms in butter with finely chopped garlic and a couple of pinches of paprika. When turning golden and releasing their juices, turn the heat down low, add sour cream or crème fraîche, chopped parsley and plenty of sea salt and black pepper. Eat with a heap of white rice.

smoked haddock with tomato and cream

Lay pieces of smoked haddock in a baking dish. Thickly slice ripe tomato and add a layer on top. Generously cover with double cream, add plenty of black pepper, and bake at 180°C/gas 4 for 15 minutes, until the fish is just cooked through.

pasta with peas and saffron

Gently fry a pinch of saffron threads in butter, with sliced spring onions and frozen petits pois. Finish with a dose of cream and toss with pasta.

meatballs

Squeeze sausages out of their skins in little balls and fry in some oil until cooked all over. In a separate pan, warm through some passata, and add the meatballs when golden. Bring to a simmer and cook for a further 20 minutes. Finally, chop in some good mozzarella, tear some basil leaves, and serve with spaghetti, plenty of Parmesan, salt and pepper.

avocado mash on toast

Mash ripe avocados with lemon or lime juice, a dash of soy sauce, best olive oil and Tabasco if you're in the mood. Scatter with sea salt and some freshly ground black pepper, and pile onto lightly toasted, thickly sliced seeded bread.

there are times when you feel like you're fighting the world. Nothing goes right, it's rained for six days running and your favourite jumper has shrunk in the wash. All you want to do is take to your bed with a boxed set of cheesy drama or lie for hours in a hot bath reading trashy magazines.

Comfort food is what you reach for at times like these. It's a nostalgic kind of eating: soothing dishes that may not be from your childhood but are certain to be from someone else's. It is the sort of food that appeals to everyone – easy to eat, straightforward to make, plain but not bland. You might eat any of them with a knife and fork, but you could manage just as well with a spoon.

The recipes in this chapter will look familiar. Here is where you'll find warming cottage pie with its pillow of smoothest mash, and tender cauliflower goldenly bubbling under a blanket of cheesy sauce. There's nothing ritzy or flashy about these dishes but, like old friends you're always pleased to see, they'll never let you down.

None of it will mend a broken heart or fix a burst pipe, but it's as close as you can get to a hug from your mum at the end of a bad day.

samuel roukin's mum's chicken soup — The ultimate
comfort food, as far as I'm concerned, is Jewish chicken soup, and this is one of
those recipes that has been passed from person to person, until it has achieved
mythical status. Bless you, Samuel Roukin's mum, wherever you are.

feeds 4 and then some

for the soup:
3 sticks celery
2 carrots, peeled
2 onions, peeled
1 plum tomato
   (tinned is fine)
2 leeks, trimmed
1 parsnip, peeled

2–3 chicken carcasses
2 sprigs thyme
Small bunch flat-leaf
   parsley
1 bay leaf
Salt and freshly ground
   black pepper
Soy sauce, to taste

for the matzo balls:
2 eggs, lightly beaten
2 tablespoons oil
2 tablespoons ice-cold
   water
70g matzo meal
½ teaspoon salt
¼ teaspoon pepper

Chop the vegetables into large chunks. Rinse the carcasses and put the soup
ingredients (except seasoning and soy sauce) into a large saucepan. Fill the pan
almost to the top with cold water and bring to the boil. Boil for up to a minute,
skimming any scum off the surface, then reduce to a simmer for 3–5 hours,
topping up with water every so often.

Meanwhile, to make the matzo balls, place all the ingredients in a large mixing
bowl and mix well. Cover and chill for at least 1 hour.

When the soup's time is up, remove the carcasses and carrots and set aside. Discard
the bay leaf and thyme stalks. Pour the soup through a sieve into a clean pan,
pushing the rest of the solid ingredients through using the back of a spoon.
Scrape the pulpy stuff off the underside of the sieve and add it to the pan.

Slice the carrots into thin sticks and remove any flesh from the chicken
carcasses. Return both the carrots and chicken flesh to the pan. Check for
seasoning, adding a few drops of soy sauce. Set aside until you are ready to eat.

Half an hour before you want to eat, bring a large pan of salted water to the
boil, and with wet hands, form balls from the matzo mixture, about 1–2cm in
diameter. Cook the balls for 30 minutes at a simmer, then drain. Reheat the
soup if it has cooled, divide the balls between bowls and ladle over the soup.

risotto milanese — Plain yet fragrant, and utterly soothing, this is Italian comfort on a plate. It is usually served as an accompaniment to osso bucco, but I like it served simply as it is in a shallow bowl, in bed or in front of the TV. You want quite a soft, runny consistency so that it's best eaten with a spoon.

If you have got a friendly butcher and feel like going the whole hog, ask for some veal or beef shin bones, sawn into pieces. Roast them for 20 minutes at 190°C/gas 5 – no need to add anything to the tin – and scoop out the meltingly delicious, rich marrow to add to the risotto.

feeds 4

100g butter, cubed
2 tablespoons olive oil
1 large onion, finely chopped
240g risotto rice
900ml best hot chicken or veal stock

1 teaspoon saffron threads, soaked in a
  little hot stock
1 small glass dry white vermouth or wine
150g grated Parmesan cheese
Salt

Heat 25g of the butter and the olive oil in a large saucepan. Fry the onion gently so that it softens without colouring – about 5–10 minutes.

Add the rice and stir around for a couple of minutes so that it is well coated in the fat. Reduce the heat, add the saffron and begin to add the stock a ladle at a time, stirring all the while. Continue to add the stock until the rice is just tender but still with a little bite; this will take about 15–20 minutes. The risotto should have a soft, creamy consistency.

Add the vermouth or wine, bubble off, then dot over the remaining butter and check for seasoning. Avoid pepper – it will overpower the delicate flavour of the saffron. Stir for a minute then spoon onto serving plates. Sprinkle with the grated Parmesan.

kipper kedgeree – Kippers make the perfect fish to put in kedgeree – smoky and fragrant, oily enough to be substantial (as well as good for you) but soft enough to flake properly. Choose fillets if you can; if you are using whole fish the picky bit of this is separating the fish from its bones and its skin.

feeds 4

2 eggs
75g butter
1 medium onion, finely chopped
¾ teaspoon hot curry powder
240g basmati rice
Pinch chilli powder (optional)

4 x 100g kipper fillets
75ml double cream
Pinch turmeric
Salt and freshly ground black pepper
Chopped flat-leaf parsley, to garnish

Place the eggs in a small pan and cover with cold water, bring to the boil and cook for 8–10 minutes, depending on how hard you like them. Remove from the pan and cool under cold, running water. Peel, quarter and set aside.

Melt the butter in a large saucepan and gently sweat the onion, so it's soft but not coloured. Add the curry powder, rice and chilli powder, if using, turning in the butter to distribute and coat. Cover with water to 1.5cm above the level of the rice. Bring to a simmer, cover and cook for 10–12 minutes until the liquid is absorbed and the rice is tender. Set aside to rest for a few minutes.

To cook the kippers, stand them upright in a jug, cover with boiling water and leave for 5 minutes.

Meanwhile, in a small pan, bring the cream and the turmeric just to the boil, then set aside.

When the fish is ready, remove from the jug and pat dry. If you have whole fish, carefully remove the skin and bones and discard; don't worry if it falls apart, you're going to break it up anyway.

Fluff up the rice, flake the fish in and check for seasoning. To serve, top with the quartered eggs and scatter the parsley over. Serve the spiced cream on the side.

potato, fontina and thyme pizzas – I've never found ready-made pizza bases to be very good. However, pitta bread, opened up, separated into two halves and brushed with olive oil makes a perfectly light, crispy replacement. The double carb hit here of white bread and potatoes is what makes this so truly comforting.

You can make another great, almost instant meal by spreading onion marmalade onto oiled bases and scattering with goats' cheese and fresh thyme.

feeds 4

240g waxy potatoes, eg Charlotte
  or Maris Peer
4 white pitta breads
Olive oil, for brushing

160g fontina or Taleggio cheese (any
  sticky, runny cheese would work fine)
2 tablespoons fresh thyme leaves
Sea salt

Preheat the oven to 180°C/gas 4.

Bring a pan of salted water to the boil, and drop in the potatoes for 5 minutes. Drain, and run under cold water until cool enough to handle.

Open up the pitta bread and separate the halves to make eight mini pizza bases, rough-side up. Paint the top of each right to the edges with a little olive oil.

Cut the cheese into thin slices and scatter over the bread. Slice the potatoes (no need to peel but discard any skin that is slipping off) as finely as you can without them falling apart and divide evenly between the pizzas. Scatter with thyme and a little salt, and bake for 10 minutes until turning golden and crispy. Either serve hot or allow to cool on a rack and serve cold.

emily's fish pie — This soothing, creamy fish pie is just what you want when you're cold inside and out. The fish is added raw to the sauce to keep it tender, and the richness is lifted by the lemon zest.

feeds 4

for the mash:
600g floury potatoes, eg Maris
   Piper, King Edward or Desiree
35g butter
100ml whole milk

for the sauce and fish:
1 small onion
1 bay leaf
500ml whole milk
40g butter

40g plain flour
Finely grated zest of ¼ unwaxed lemon
1 tablespoon chopped fresh tarragon leaves
3 tablespoons chopped flat-leaf parsley
200g smoked fish, eg smoked haddock
400g firm white fish, eg pollack or coley
200g frozen North Atlantic prawns, thawed
Sea salt and freshly ground black pepper
Peas, to serve

For the mash, peel and cut the potatoes. Then cook in lightly salted boiling water until tender. Drain and return to the pan, allowing the steam to drift off and the potatoes to dry. Mash the butter and milk into the potatoes. The mash should be firm, not sloppy.

Preheat the oven to 180°C/gas 4.

For the white sauce, peel the onion and cut in half, and place in a pan with the bay leaf and the milk. Bring to a gentle simmer, put aside to infuse for about 15 minutes and then strain.

Melt the butter in a pan and add the flour when it starts to foam. Cook, stirring constantly for a minute. Gradually add the strained milk, stirring constantly to form a thick sauce. Stir in the lemon zest, tarragon and parsley and season well.

Cut the fish into bite-sized pieces and place in a baking dish along with the prawns. Pour over the white sauce, mixing it around all of the fish. Top with the mashed potato and place in the oven until golden on top, about 40 minutes.

Serve with peas, and some bread, if you like.

pappardelle with caramelised pork

— This is a variation on the classic Italian dish of pork loin braised in milk – as the milk reduces and combines with the lemon oils, it becomes sticky and caramelised, lending a wonderful sweetness to the dish. I like it with pappardelle, but you could just as well eat it with mash for a really homely dish.

feeds 4

Olive oil, for frying
600g pork mince
1 large onion, finely chopped
Finely grated zest of 1 unwaxed
  lemon
2 bay leaves
200ml whole milk

3 tablespoons finely grated Parmesan
  cheese
4 tablespoons double cream
400g pappardelle
Knob of butter
Salt and freshly ground black pepper

Preheat the oven to 160°C/gas 3.

Heat a little olive oil in a flameproof casserole, add the mince, season it and break it up into small bits so that it turns very golden in places, not just lightly coloured. After 5 minutes, add the onion and cook for a further 10 minutes. Pour off any watery liquid as you go (pork has a tendency to this).

When the meat is golden and the onion soft and sweet, add the lemon zest, bay leaves and milk. The milk should come up the sides of the mince but not cover it. Bring to the boil, then cover.

Bake in the oven for 1½–2 hours until the milk has evaporated and the meat is tender and sweet. If there is still any watery liquid left, uncover and reduce it on the hob. Season to taste.

Mash together the Parmesan and cream and season generously.

When you are ready to eat, cook the pasta in plenty of well-salted, boiling water according to the packet instructions, until al dente, then drain, and add a knob of butter. Toss the meat and the creamy Parmesan mixture through the pasta, and eat straight away.

cauliflower cheese with bacon and breadcrumbs

I've made this traditional nursery dish more substantial by adding bacon and breadcrumbs, but you could just make it plain. The key is to make sure the cauliflower is properly tender rather than al dente.

feeds 4

2 heads cauliflower
1 onion
1 clove
1 bay leaf
1 litre whole milk
60g butter

60g plain flour
350g mature Cheddar cheese, grated
200g lardons or chopped bacon
2 handfuls of fresh breadcrumbs
Salt and freshly ground black pepper

Preheat the oven to 200°C/gas 6.

Cut each cauliflower into 6–8 wedges, and boil or steam until tender – about 8–10 minutes. Drain and transfer to a gratin dish. Set aside.

To make the cheese sauce, peel the onion and cut in half, stud with the clove and place in a pan with the bay leaf and the milk. Bring to a gentle simmer, put aside to infuse for 15 minutes and then strain.

Melt the butter in a large pan and add the flour when it starts to foam. Cook, stirring constantly for about 5 minutes. Gradually add the strained milk over a low heat, stirring constantly to form a satiny white sauce. If there are any lumps, you can take a hand-held electric blender to it, which should sort it out. Add the cheese and stir until smooth. Pour the sauce over the cauliflower.

Fry the lardons in a small pan – you shouldn't need any extra fat – until they turn golden. Add the breadcrumbs, stirring briefly to coat in the bacon juices. Scatter the lardons and crumbs over the cauliflower cheese and bake for 10 minutes until golden and bubbling.

macaroni cheese — There are times when nothing but macaroni cheese will do – it's a 'run me a bath and take me to bed' kind of supper. Here, the golden sage on top gives it a delicately scented crispy topping.

feeds 4

300g macaroni
1 onion
1 clove
1 bay leaf
750ml milk
60g butter
50g plain flour

3 tablespoons double cream
200g mature Cheddar cheese, grated
100g Taleggio cheese, peeled and cubed

75g Parmesan cheese, grated
10 sage leaves
Salt and freshly ground black pepper

Cook the macaroni in plenty of salted boiling water according to the packet instructions, but take it off the heat a couple of minutes before the specified cooking time. Drain and rinse with cold water to stop it from cooking further.

For the cheese sauce, peel the onion and cut in half, stud with the clove and place in a pan with the bay leaf and milk. Bring to a gentle simmer, put aside to infuse for 15 minutes and then strain.

Melt 50g of the butter in a large pan and add the flour when it starts to foam. Cook, stirring constantly, for about 5 minutes. Gradually add the strained milk, stirring all the time, to form a satiny white sauce that just coats the back of a spoon. If any lumps remain, blend till smooth with a hand-held electric blender.

Add the cream, Cheddar, Taleggio and half the Parmesan and stir, over a very low heat, until smooth.

Add the pasta to the sauce and warm through. Don't worry if it seems like there is too much sauce; some will be absorbed by the pasta. Season very well, being particularly generous with the black pepper.

Preheat the grill to high. Transfer the pasta and sauce to a gratin dish and scatter with the remaining Parmesan. Lay over the sage leaves in a flower pattern. Put a little dot of the remaining butter over each leaf then grill for 6–7 minutes, until golden and bubbling.

burger with balsamic onions — A burger needn't come with a

bun; it's much more comforting on a pillow of mash. Don't forget the ketchup.

feeds 4

4 red onions
2 tablespoons sunflower oil
2 tablespoons good olive oil
2 tablespoons good balsamic vinegar
2 teaspoons light brown muscovado sugar

600g beef mince
Salt and freshly ground black pepper
Smooth mash (p.272) and tomato
  ketchup, to serve

First, peel and halve the onions, then slice finely into semicircles. Warm the sunflower oil and half the olive oil in a saucepan over a high heat and add the onions. Once sizzling, reduce the heat to low and cook for 20–30 minutes, stirring from time to time.

After 10 minutes, add the vinegar and sugar, and cook on until soft and sweet.

Stir the remaining olive oil through the mince, seasoning enthusiastically, and shape the meat into four 2cm-thick patties. Skim off a couple of tablespoons of the onion oil and paint over the beef patties.

Heat a griddle pan to very hot and cook the meat for 3 minutes or so on each side, for something between rare and medium-rare.

Spoon the onions onto 4 plates with a slotted spoon, leaving any surplus oil behind, and top with the steak. Serve with mash and ketchup.

twice-baked cottage pie – This recipe has taken me years to hone and I am very attached to it. The key to its amazing tenderness is in the oven baking, rather than stove-top simmering. To use this method, start cooking the day before you want to eat.

makes 2 pies, each for 4 people (one for now and one for the freezer)

Olive oil, for frying
1kg beef mince
3 medium onions, finely chopped
2 medium carrots, finely chopped
2 celery sticks, finely chopped
150g lardons or chopped bacon
6 medium garlic cloves
3 bay leaves
4–5 sprigs rosemary and/or thyme
200ml milk
1 large glass red wine

2 tablespoons pomegranate molasses
   or tomato ketchup
Dash of Worcestershire sauce
2 teaspoons Dijon mustard
Salt and freshly ground black pepper
Peas, to serve

for the mash:
1.2kg floury potatoes, eg Maris Piper,
   King Edward or Desiree
80g butter
100ml whole milk

Preheat the oven to 160°C/gas 3. Heat a couple of tablespoons of oil in a large frying pan over a high heat and begin to fry the meat in batches. Leave it for a couple of minutes before turning and breaking it up so that it not only colours but begins to turn golden and caramelise.

At the same time, heat 3 tablespoons of olive oil in a large flameproof casserole and fry the onion, carrot and celery until it softens, for about 5 minutes, stirring to prevent burning. Next add the lardons or bacon, stir and fry for 5 minutes. Peel and smash the garlic cloves and add them to the casserole with the herbs. At this stage you may need to add a bit more oil.

After 15 minutes, when the vegetables are soft, golden and sticky, add the browned mince. Deglaze the frying pan with a splash of water, and add to the casserole, along with the milk. Turn the heat up and bubble for a couple of minutes until most of the liquid boils away. Add the wine, molasses or ketchup, a slug of Worcestershire sauce and the mustard, bring to the boil, put the lid on and transfer to the oven. *(Continued overleaf.)*

Bake for 1½ hours, stirring once half way through, and adding more wine or water if it looks too dry.

After 1½ hours, stir again, taste for seasoning (the lardons should preclude any need for salt) then return to the oven. Switch the oven off and allow the meat to cool slowly overnight.

In the morning, scrape off surplus fat which will have hardened, and remove whatever is left of the herbs that you can easily dig out. Transfer the meat to 2 pie dishes or separate into whatever portions suit you best. If you are freezing any of the cooked meat, transfer to lidded airtight containers, label it clearly and freeze.

For the mash, peel and cut the potatoes. Then cook in lightly salted boiling water until tender. Drain and return to the pan, allowing the steam to drift off and the potatoes to dry.

Preheat the oven to 180°C/gas 4.

Mash the butter and milk into the potatoes – you want the mash to be firm, not sloppy. Check for seasoning, spread over the meat, making rivulets with the tines of a fork, and give one last grind of salt and pepper.

Bake the pie in the preheated oven for 45–60 minutes, until piping hot inside, golden brown on top and the meat is bubbling up at the sides.

Serve the pie with peas.

butter chicken — This curry all-rounder has just the right balance of sweetness and spice, flavour, richness and comfort, and enough of a kick to perk you up. You can also make it very successfully with leftover cooked chicken: simply add 150–200g meat per person to the cooked sauce and heat through until piping hot.

feeds 4

4–6 chicken thigh fillets, skinned
Vegetable oil, for frying
1 large red onion, finely chopped
5cm piece fresh root ginger, peeled
 and finely chopped
2 garlic cloves, chopped
1 green chilli, deseeded and finely
 chopped
1 tablespoon ground coriander
1 scant teaspoon hot chilli powder
1 teaspoon garam masala

Pinch turmeric
400g tin chopped tomatoes
500–600ml chicken stock
100g butter
8 curry leaves
50–75g ground almonds
75–100g plain yoghurt
Salt and freshly ground black pepper
Basmati rice, poppadoms, naan, Raita
 (p.191) and mango chutney, to serve

Cut the chicken into strips. Heat a little oil in a flameproof casserole or large saucepan, and brown the chicken all over, then set aside.

Add the onion to the casserole or pan and fry over a medium-high heat, adding more oil if necessary, stirring until it begins to colour, about 7–8 minutes.

Meanwhile, pound the ginger, garlic and green chilli into a paste and add it to the onion for the last couple of minutes. Add the spices, and fry on for a minute. Season and add the tomatoes, and cook for 5 minutes.

Add 500ml of the stock, the butter and curry leaves, bring to the boil, and simmer with the lid off for about 15 minutes to allow the spices to temper and infuse, and the liquid to reduce a little. Add enough almonds and yoghurt until you have the desired consistency.

Finally, return the chicken to the pan, simmering until just cooked, and make any last-minute adjustments – more yoghurt will calm the spices, more almonds will thicken, more stock will thin. Eat with basmati rice and whatever extras take your fancy.

sausage cassoulet — You could easily double the quantities here for a winter feast – great for Bonfire Night or Hallowe'en. It's extremely hearty, so a peppery green salad is all you'll need on the side.

If you don't want to soak the beans yourself, or can't start the night before, replace them with 2 tins of drained beans on the day.

feeds 4

275g dried cannellini or haricot beans
2 tablespoons olive oil
8 good-quality chunky pork sausages
160g smoked pancetta, cut into 1cm strips
2 onions, roughly chopped

6 garlic cloves, peeled and flattened
227g tin chopped tomatoes
2 bay leaves
2 sprigs thyme
½ teaspoon paprika
¼ teaspoon ground coriander

1 heaped tablespoon soft dark brown sugar
600ml boiling water
60g fresh white breadcrumbs
Peppery green salad leaves, to serve

Put the dried beans in a large bowl and cover with cold water. Set aside, and leave to soak overnight.

The next day, when you are ready to cook, discard any discoloured beans or ones that float to the top, drain and set aside.

Preheat the oven to 140°C/gas 1.

Heat the olive oil in a flameproof casserole and fry the sausages and pancetta until golden and well coloured; set aside.

Add the onions to the casserole and cook for 5–10 minutes until softened and golden. Add the garlic a few minutes before the end.

Return the sausages and pancetta to the casserole and add the remaining ingredients, apart from the breadcrumbs. Bring just to the boil, cover and bake for 2 hours. Check occasionally to make sure it's not drying out and add more water if necessary.

After 2 hours, remove the lid, sprinkle over the breadcrumbs and bake for a further hour until the beans are tender and the top is golden and crunchy.

Serve with a peppery green salad.

weekend food

weekend food ... in a rush

chickpea and feta salad

Drain a can of chickpeas, break up a packet of feta and combine with half a finely chopped preserved lemon, a small red chilli, and a pinch of dried mint. Drench with olive oil and allow to marinate for as long as you can. This will keep for a couple of weeks in a sealed glass jar, in the fridge, if it is covered in oil. Eat scattered with parsley or fresh mint, or add to any salad leaves.

chorizo with lentils

Cut chorizo into rounds on the diagonal, and fry, with some chopped onion, until golden. Add cooked Puy lentils (the ready-cooked vacuum-packed ones are fine), a good slug of beer, and bring to a simmer, uncovered, for 5 or so minutes. Scatter with chopped parsley, and eat with all the juices, and a rocket and tomato salad.

warm wilted frisée, feta and beetroot salad

Wash the leaves, then turn, still damp, into a saucepan with olive oil, lay over a block of feta, cover and cook for 5 minutes. Serve with boiled or roasted beetroot.

pasta with anchovy, broccoli and chilli

Separate broccoli, or better still, purple sprouting broccoli into small heads, blanch in salted boiling water, then drain. Fry together anchovy fillets and finely chopped chilli and garlic for a couple of minutes in olive oil, then stir in the broccoli. Toss through buttered, al dente pasta and eat with plenty of Parmesan.

self-assembly blats

Lay out on a board: buttered white bread, crispy lettuce leaves like Iceberg or Little Gem, sliced beefsteak tomatoes, sliced avocados, a bowl of mayonnaise and one of ketchup. Fry the best bacon you can get your hands on until golden and not quite crispy, and allow everyone to make up their own version of a perfect sandwich.

Weekends make me long for the country – blustery walks in sun or rain, silly games, and, season notwithstanding, a fire in the evening with lots of red wine to drink by it. The pace slows down. There's time to digest the week, ruminate over the papers, potter about a bit. And then there's the cooking. Weekends, particularly the inclement sort – as likely in summer as winter – are made for it.

The difference with weekend food is that you don't have to rush at it. Rooting around independent shops to seek out the best of the season becomes a pleasure; the timetable for meals is more elastic. Big, rustic flavours can take their time to settle in together, tougher cuts of meat can relax over the course of several hours.

It's the sort of cooking that demands something from you only at the start – chopping, sweating, browning – and then takes care of itself. These are dishes that emerge from the kitchen with some fanfare: unctuous, hearty stews and golden, crackling roasts. Their big, intense flavours demand your full attention and need very little in terms of accessorising – a few potatoes or some fresh bread, vegetables at their best, simply cooked.

Not every meal has to shine. One of the best things about producing one glorious dish is that the rest of the day can be taken care of by soups, leftovers and assembled plates of deli fare. The kitchen needs a break, too.

four stews

lamb stew with tomatoes, chickpeas and rice

This dish is one of my favourites – the lamb melts into the tomato, becoming extremely tender, whilst the chickpeas give it a nutty bite.

You don't really need to add anything to this to make it a complete meal but occasionally I serve it with a green salad, which I generally eat afterwards off the same plate, to mop up the juices.

feeds 4

600g stewing lamb, diced into 3–4cm cubes
5 tablespoons olive oil
2 garlic cloves, finely chopped
400g tin chopped tomatoes
3 sprigs rosemary

500ml chicken stock
175g brown basmati rice
300g tinned, drained chickpeas
Salt and freshly ground black pepper
Good old green salad (p.271), to serve

Season the lamb. Heat the oil in a large pan and brown the lamb all over. Add the garlic, stir around for a minute, then add the tomatoes and rosemary and enough stock to cover the meat. Bring to a simmer and cook, covered, for 1½ hours, checking there's enough liquid from time to time, and topping up if necessary.

Add the remaining stock, 400ml water, the rice and chickpeas, and seasoning. Bring back to a simmer for a further 30 minutes. Serve as it is, or with a green salad.

braised venison with thyme and beetroot — I love

the deep purplish colours of this stew – the method is simple but the flavours are wonderfully complex, with the savouriness of the meat, the sweetness of the beetroot and the heat of the chilli (if you choose to use it).

feeds 4

Olive oil, for frying
600g venison, diced into 3–4cm cubes
100g streaky bacon or pancetta, diced into 1cm pieces
1 large onion, chopped
4 sprigs thyme

1 dried bird's-eye chilli (optional)
2 large glasses dry red wine, eg Chianti
4 medium beetroot, topped, tailed and quartered
Salt and freshly ground black pepper
White rice and green salad leaves, to serve

Preheat the oven to 180°C/gas 4.

Warm a couple of tablespoons of oil in a flameproof casserole and fry the venison and bacon over a medium heat until turning golden. Remove the venison and bacon to a plate and set aside.

Reduce the heat, add the onion and thyme and crumble the chilli, if using, into the casserole. Cook until the onion is soft and translucent but do not let it burn.

Return the meat to the casserole, add the wine and beetroot and bring to the boil, simmering for 5 minutes until the alcohol has burnt off. Season to taste, being generous with the black pepper, cover and cook in the oven for 1½ hours.

Serve simply with rice and peppery green salad leaves such as rocket or watercress.

slow-cooked beef shin stew — This is a perfect stew to make when you're mooching around on a cold weekend, and have time to go to the butcher to get this great value cut of meat. I always double the volume as it's very versatile, and once the bigger bits of meat have all been fished out, the leftover sauce goes as well with a crunchy baked potato as it does with large shell pasta (conchiglie).

feeds 4

Olive oil, for frying
2 medium onions, chopped
2 medium carrots, chopped
1 stick celery, sliced
4 garlic cloves, pressed under a knife
  and peeled
2 bay leaves
600g beef shin, cut into 1.5cm cubes

1 large glass dry red wine, eg Chianti
250ml good stock
400g tin chopped tomatoes
2 sprigs rosemary
1 tablespoon pomegranate molasses
  (optional)
Salt and freshly ground black pepper

Preheat the oven to 140°C/gas 1.

Heat a generous amount of oil in a flameproof casserole and fry the onions, carrots, celery, garlic and bay leaves, stirring for 5 minutes, then reduce the heat, cover and continue to sweat them for a further 10–15 minutes.

Meanwhile, season the cubes of meat. Heat a couple of tablespoons of olive oil in a large frying pan, and brown the meat over a high heat until it has a good colour all over. You may need to do this in batches so you don't overcrowd the pan. Set each batch aside in a bowl, deglazing the pan between batches with a little of the wine, if it looks like the delicious brown bits left behind are starting to turn black and bitter. Add the deglazing liquid to the browned meat.

Once all the meat is browned and the vegetables in the casserole are softened, add the meat to the casserole, with the remaining wine, stock, tomatoes, rosemary and pomegranate molasses, if using.

Bring to a boil to bubble off the alcohol for a couple of minutes, then cover and put in the oven. Cook for 3–4 hours – it's a pretty good-humoured stew once the connective tissues in the meat have had a chance to melt away, so you can eat it whenever, and with whatever you like.

vegetable stew with saffron and parsley pistou

This recipe is made for summer vegetables, but you could easily make it in winter, with the alternative list of ingredients below, cooking until the root veg are tender.

feeds 4

3 tablespoons olive oil
1 red pepper, deseeded and thinly sliced
1 onion, thinly sliced
1 bay leaf
Good pinch saffron threads
8–12 small waxy potatoes
600ml boiling water
Buttered sourdough toast, to serve

for the summer stew:
2 large ripe tomatoes, deseeded and
  chopped
1 fennel bulb, thinly sliced
2 small new carrots, diced
2 small courgettes, diced
175g green beans, chopped into
  5cm lengths
175g shelled baby broad beans or peas

for the winter stew:
2 tinned plum tomatoes, chopped
¼ celeriac, diced
1 parsnip, diced
1 large winter carrot, diced
400g tin cannellini or haricot blanc beans,
  drained

for the pistou:
2 garlic cloves, peeled
Leaves from 1 large bunch flat-leaf
  parsley, finely chopped
5 tablespoons olive oil
Salt and freshly ground black pepper

Warm the olive oil in a large pan. Add the red pepper, onion, bay leaf and saffron, and stew gently without letting them colour until they go very soft, stirring regularly to prevent sticking and burning. This will take about 25 minutes.

To make the pistou, pound the garlic cloves with a pinch of salt to form a paste. Stir the parsley into the garlic paste and gradually add the oil. Set aside.

Add the potatoes and boiling water to the onion, along with the tomatoes. Bring to the boil, then reduce to simmer for 10 minutes. Add the fennel, carrots, courgettes and green beans and simmer for 5 minutes. Season to taste, then add the broad beans or peas and bring just back to a blip.

Stir a tablespoon of pistou into the stew and divide the stew between soup bowls. Serve with buttered toast on the side and the rest of the pistou in a bowl.

a handful of roasts

garlic and thyme roast chicken — This is a buttery,
celebratory kind of roast chicken, packed with the herby flavours of summer
and just right for any occasion.

feeds 4

2 heads garlic, plus 3 peeled and
   finely chopped garlic cloves
1 medium free-range chicken,
   approximately 1.5kg
25g thyme sprigs
1 lemon, halved

40g unsalted butter, at room temperature
½ bottle good white wine
Sea salt and freshly ground black pepper
Fresh herb and lemon salad (p.271),
   French beans with lardons (p.270) and
   your favourite potatoes, to serve

Preheat the oven to 220°C/gas 7.

Cut the tops off the garlic heads to expose the cloves and stuff into each end
of the chicken, along with half the thyme sprigs. Squeeze the juice from each
lemon half into each end and stuff the rest of the lemon inside, too.

Strip the leaves from the remaining thyme sprigs. Pound the thyme leaves and
the chopped garlic cloves into the butter, and smear it generously all over the
chicken. Season generously with plenty of sea salt and black pepper. Place the
chicken in a large roasting tray and pour the wine into the tray. There should
be about 2.5cm of liquid; top up with water if necessary.

Roast for 20 minutes, then reduce the temperature to 190°C/gas 5 and continue
to cook for a further 40–50 minutes. Keep an eye on the liquid in the bottom of
the tray, topping up with water if necessary (this makes an instant gravy at the end).

Check the chicken is cooked by piercing the thigh with a sharp knife or skewer;
the juices should run clear, not pink. Remove from the roasting tin and set aside
to rest for 15 minutes.

Skim any surplus fat off the cooking juices and transfer to a jug. Carve the
chicken and serve with the instant gravy, salad, French beans and potatoes.

rare beef fillet with horseradish sauce — Although

breathtakingly expensive, this is ideal for any special occasion, is no last-minute sweat, and looks beautiful on the table (see overleaf). The meat will be quite tepid by the time you come to eat it, but meltingly tender. Serve with the horseradish sauce below, and/or Salsa verde (p.273).

feeds 4–8, with generous leftovers if serving 4

1 whole beef fillet,
  about 1.5kg
2 beetroot
2 red onions
4 heads garlic
12 new potatoes
Olive oil, for drizzling
4 sprigs rosemary

1 large fennel bulb
4 small courgettes,
  halved diagonally
12 cherry tomatoes on
  the vine
Sea salt and freshly ground
  black pepper

for the horseradish sauce:
50g fresh horseradish,
  peeled and finely grated
1 teaspoon sherry vinegar
½ teaspoon English
  mustard
Pinch sugar
75g crème fraîche

Preheat the oven to 240°C/gas 9.

Lay out 2 sheets of foil, in a roasting tin, large enough to completely enclose the meat once it is cooked. Place the beef in the tin. When the oven is as hot as it can be, roast the meat, unwrapped, for 22 minutes exactly. Remove from the oven, wrap the meat loosely in the foil, seal it firmly and leave to sit somewhere warm (I find just next to the oven is fine) for 1–2 hours. Meanwhile, reduce the oven temperature to 180°C/gas 4.

Top and tail the beetroot, and chop in half if large. Peel and quarter the onions. Cut the tops off the garlic heads to expose a little of the cloves. Place the beetroot, onions, garlic and new potatoes in a second large roasting tin, turn them in olive oil, scrunch over plenty of sea salt and pepper, lay over the rosemary sprigs and roast for 45 minutes.

Top, tail and cut the fennel into wedges. Blanch the fennel wedges in boiling water for 2 minutes and add to the vegetables, with the courgettes, after 15 minutes. After a further 15 minutes add the cherry tomatoes. Roast, turning from time to time, until tender and beginning to turn golden, about another 15 minutes. Remove from the oven and again leave the tin somewhere warm, until you are ready to eat.

To make the sauce, mix the grated horseradish, vinegar, mustard, sugar and a pinch of salt together. Let them sit and breathe with each other for a few minutes – it's a pretty powerful set of characters. Finally, stir in the crème fraîche. This sauce will keep for a few days in the fridge.

When you are ready to eat, carve the meat into slices. Pile the vegetables up high on a platter in a jumble, or separate into different corners if you think you have a few fussy eaters. Serve alongside the meat and whatever sauce you choose.

very slow roast shoulder of pork with rhubarb

The extremely slow, long cooking of the pork renders the meat meltingly tender. The rhubarb here replaces the traditional apple sauce as a taste that cuts through the rich meat. This will make too much for 4, but there is plenty to do with leftovers: stuffed between slices of bread for the best sandwich, shredded into stir fries and even added to baked beans.

feeds 4 plus leftovers

½ pork shoulder on the bone
  (about 2.5–4kg)
3 large garlic cloves, peeled
3cm piece fresh root ginger, peeled
1 teaspoon dried chilli flakes
1 teaspoon ground ginger
2 teaspoons five-spice powder
2 teaspoons brown sugar
1 teaspoon flaky salt

1 teaspoon sunflower or groundnut oil
2 teaspoons soy sauce
Noodles or Smooth mash (p.272),
  to serve

for the rhubarb sauce:
450g rhubarb, cut into 4cm pieces
150–200g caster sugar
1 small glass dry white wine

Score the rind of the pork shoulder with a very sharp knife (a Stanley knife works very well) in parallel lines about 1cm apart, to a depth of 1cm. Alternatively ask your butcher to do this.

Grate the garlic and fresh ginger into a small bowl and mix to a paste with the chilli flakes, ground ginger, five-spice powder, brown sugar, salt, oil and soy sauce.

Preheat the oven to 230°C/gas 8. Place the pork shoulder, skin-side up, on a rack above a large roasting tin. Rub half the spice paste into the scored rind of the pork and roast for 30 minutes.

Then remove from the oven and, very carefully, using a cloth or oven gloves as the meat will be very hot, turn the joint over. Smear the remainder of the spice paste over the underside (now on top) of the meat with a spoon.

Add 250ml water to the tin, turn the oven down to 110°C/gas ¼ and return the joint to the oven. Leave for anything from 10–14 hours, turning it skin-side up again, and basting with the fat and juices in the tin, about half way through the cooking time.

Meanwhile, to make the rhubarb sauce: put all the ingredients in a pan over a medium heat, and simmer, mostly covered, until the rhubarb is completely tender and falling apart. Remove from the heat, stir, and set aside to cool (the sauce is served at room temperature).

About 45 minutes before you want to eat, turn the oven right up to 230°C/gas 8 to crisp up the crackling. Keep an eye on it to make sure it doesn't burn.

To serve the pork, remove the crackled skin in a single piece and break it up to share. Divide the tender meat up by simply pulling it apart. Serve with the crackling, rhubarb sauce and noodles or mash.

honey rose ham

honey rose ham — This ham is scented with dried rose petals, which is a very old-fashioned English treatment for it. It is just as delicious served hot or cold, and feeds more than 4, but leftovers last for a good week, well wrapped, in the fridge, and there's plenty to do with them. I like to serve slices of the ham with fried eggs, chop it and mix with pasta and cream or add to soups and risottos.

feeds 4 plus leftovers

2kg smoked or unsmoked gammon joint
1 litre apple juice or dry cider
6 whole black peppercorns
1 bay leaf
2 tablespoons dried edible rose petals
Grated zest of ½ unwaxed lemon
2 tablespoons coriander seeds

2 tablespoons fennel seeds
Seeds from 8 cardamom pods
4 tablespoons clear honey
12 cloves
Perfect baked potatoes (p.272) and
   Good old green salad (p.271), to serve

Place the gammon in a large pan, cover it with water, bring to the boil and then drain and discard the water.

Now add the apple juice or cider, peppercorns and bay leaf, and top up with water so the ham is completely covered. Bring to the boil, then simmer for 1 hour 40 minutes (or 20 minutes per 450g). Set aside, in the cooking liquid, until it is cool enough to handle (or leave to stand overnight in the cooking liquid until completely cool if you like). Discard the liquid or reserve to use as stock for a leftover ham risotto.

Preheat the oven to 220°C/gas 7.

Carefully cut off the rind and discard, making sure to leave a layer of fat on the meat. Score across in 1.5cm diamonds. Pound together the rose petals, lemon zest and all the spices, apart from the cloves, until they are ground down, then stir in the honey until well amalgamated. Spread the spiced honey over the surface of the ham, then stud it at regular intervals with the cloves. Bake for 10–15 minutes, basting once or twice until turning golden and glazed.

Eat warm from the oven or cold anytime, with baked potatoes and salad.

roast root vegetable salad – This is brilliant served instead of or alongside a roast, negating the need for any other side. It looks after vegetarians well, too.

feeds 4

for the salad:
2 red onions, peeled and cut into wedges
2 parsnips, peeled and cut into
   1.5cm chunks
1 small butternut squash, peeled and
   cut into 1.5cm chunks
2 medium or 4 small beetroot, topped
   and tailed and cut into 1.5cm chunks
2 small or 1 large sweet potato, peeled
   and cut into 1.5cm chunks
4 garlic cloves, unpeeled
Olive oil, for coating
4 sprigs rosemary

75g pine nuts
200g rocket
100g feta cheese
Salt and freshly ground black pepper

for the dressing:
3 tablespoons rapeseed oil or
   extra virgin olive oil
1 tablespoon cider vinegar
1 teaspoon Dijon mustard
Generous pinch flaky salt
Freshly ground black pepper

Preheat the oven to 180°C/gas 4.

Place the prepared vegetables and garlic in a roasting tray, toss in olive oil and season generously. Add the rosemary sprigs and roast for 35–40 minutes, turning once or twice. Add the pine nuts 10 minutes before the end.

Place the dressing ingredients in a small jug, season well with freshly ground black pepper and stir well to combine.

Once the vegetables are cooked, discard the rosemary stalks. Toss the roasted vegetables with the rocket and crumble the feta over the top.

Give the dressing a good stir and drizzle it over the top of the salad to serve.

three rustic soups

ewa's polish sausage soup – Our friend Ewa makes this very simple soup through the winter, and it's sturdy and reliably delicious. Its flavour comes from the smoked Polish sausage, now widely available in supermarkets.

feeds 4

200g smoked Polish sausage
100g pancetta
350g floury potatoes, eg Maris Piper, King Edward or Desiree, peeled and roughly chopped
1 large carrot, finely chopped
1 parsnip, finely chopped

150g yellow split peas
1 bay leaf
½ tablespoon dried marjoram
600ml chicken stock
1 tablespoon vegetable oil
Freshly ground black pepper

Chop the sausage and pancetta into 1.5cm pieces. Put all the ingredients into a large pan and simmer together for 1 hour, until soft, and the split peas are starting to collapse.

You may want to season with some black pepper, but the smoked meat should contribute enough salt.

minestrone — This is as hearty and warming a soup as you could ask for. It improves over a couple of days, so it is well worth doubling the quantities.

If you have a block of Parmesan in your fridge, cut off the hard rind and throw it in too – it adds a wonderful flavour. In fact, next time you get to the end of a wedge of Parmesan, wrap the rind in foil and instead of throwing it away, freeze for when you make this soup.

feeds 4

30g butter
4 tablespoons extra virgin olive oil
2 onions, finely chopped
2 large carrots, diced
2 sticks celery, diced
6 garlic cloves, peeled and squashed
  under the blade of a knife
1 large potato, diced
1 medium courgette, diced
1.5 litres vegetable stock or water

Parmesan rind (optional)
400g tin cannellini beans, drained
  and rinsed
200g cavolo nero or savoy cabbage,
  shredded
75g spaghetti, broken up
Sea salt and freshly ground black pepper
Extra virgin olive oil or Classic pesto
  (p.273) and grated Parmesan cheese,
  to serve

Heat the butter and oil together in a large flameproof casserole, add all the chopped vegetables, apart from the cavolo nero, and with the lid on, sweat together, for 10–15 minutes, stirring a couple of times. You do not want them to stick or colour.

Add the stock or water and Parmesan rind, if using. Bring to the boil, reduce to a simmer and cook at a mere blip for 1½–2 hours, topping up with water if necessary.

Add the cannellini beans and cavolo nero, season to taste and cook for a further 30 minutes.

Finally, add the spaghetti and cook for 15 minutes.

Serve with a swirl of best olive oil and/or a little fresh pesto stirred through and freshly grated Parmesan on top.

chorizo, chickpea and kale soup — More often than

not, this soup is lunch on Saturday. It's very quick and simple to make and wonderfully robust and tasty.

feeds 4

Olive oil, for frying
250g chorizo sausage, diagonally sliced
    to the thickness of a pound coin
200g floury potatoes, eg Maris Piper,
    King Edward or Desiree, peeled and
    roughly chopped
1 onion, roughly chopped

400g tin chickpeas
Splash of white wine, beer or cider
    (optional)
100g kale, roughly chopped
Salt and freshly ground black pepper
Extra virgin olive oil, for drizzling

Heat a little olive oil in a large pan, sweat the chorizo, potato and onion in the oil until the onion is soft and translucent, the sausage is releasing its spicy orange oils and the potato is beginning to soften but not colour.

Add the chickpea liquid and enough water (with a splash of white wine, beer or cider if you have it to hand) to cover the contents of the pan by about 1cm. Half cover with a lid, and simmer for 30 minutes.

Add the chickpeas and kale and simmer for another 10 minutes. Check for seasoning and serve with a generous dose of your best olive oil.

a summer risotto, a winter risotto and one from the store cupboard

courgette and goats' cheese risotto — This risotto is the essence of summer, with the delicate, creamy flavours of courgette and goats' cheese sharpened by peppery, floral basil. Perfect for a low-key supper in the garden as the light fades away.

feeds 4

3 medium or 5 small courgettes
40g butter
3 tablespoons olive oil
2 red onions, finely chopped
250g risotto rice
900ml hot chicken stock

Small glass white wine or vermouth
150g creamy goats' cheese, crumbled
Handful of torn basil leaves
Extra virgin olive oil, for drizzling
Salt and freshly ground black pepper

Grate the courgettes on the coarse side of a box grater. Spread out into a large sieve, sprinkle some salt over and leave to drain for 30 minutes. Rinse thoroughly and pat dry.

Heat the butter and olive oil in a large pan and fry the onions until they are translucent but not coloured, about 5 minutes over a medium heat. Add the grated courgettes and stir until they are coated in oil. Now add the rice and stir until it is coated too.

Add the hot stock, ladle by ladle, as the rice absorbs it, stirring all the while. It should take 15–20 minutes until completely cooked – the rice should be soft but still retain a little bite, and have a creamy, dropping consistency. When the rice is nearly tender, add the wine and bubble off for a minute.

At the last minute, stir through the goats' cheese (it doesn't have to melt right through) and the torn basil leaves. Serve drizzled with a little extra virgin olive oil and sprinkled with some black pepper – no need for Parmesan here; the flavour is too delicate to support it.

lentil and smoked bacon brown rice risotto

This risotto is so hearty it might have come from some lost Alpine village. I often make it with leftover roast chicken gravy, which is basically a very rich stock. If you are working from a stock cube add some butter to emulate the extra richness.

feeds 4

40g butter
1 tablespoon olive oil
2 medium onions, coarsely chopped
100g smoked bacon or pancetta
2 garlic cloves, finely chopped
200g wholegrain rice
150g Puy lentils
1 small glass Riesling or medium white wine

900ml very rich hot chicken stock, including leftover gravy or 1 chicken stock cube, made up with 900ml water, plus 25g butter
100g Reblochon cheese, rind removed, cubed
Sea salt and freshly ground black pepper
Grated Parmesan cheese, to serve

In a heavy-based pan, heat the butter and olive oil together, and fry the onions fairly gently, stirring to prevent sticking, until soft but not coloured (about 5 minutes). Next add the bacon and continue to cook, so both become soft without colouring. Add the garlic and fry for 1 minute.

Add the rice and lentils, stir to coat in the oil and butter, then add the white wine. Bring to the boil and allow to bubble off, stirring, until almost all the liquid has been absorbed.

Now begin to add your hot stock, about a third at a time, stirring as you do, so that the rice can break down evenly. Once all the liquid has been nearly absorbed (about 25–30 minutes), taste to check texture and seasoning – it should still have bite but not crunch, so if it is not yet cooked, continue by adding water from a boiled kettle.

When the risotto is cooked, if you are using chicken stock from a cube, stir in the butter at this stage. Stir in the Reblochon, leaving the Parmesan for people to help themselves.

store-cupboard risotto — The ingredients here come almost entirely from longer lasting provisions but the end result is deliciously bright in colour and fresh in flavour. If you don't have (or can't get) any cream, stir in an extra knob of butter instead.

feeds 4

2 tablespoons olive oil
25g butter
2 shallots or 1 medium onion, finely chopped
250g risotto rice
900ml hot chicken or vegetable stock
10 cubes frozen spinach
150g frozen petits pois

1 garlic clove, peeled
70ml double cream (or an extra knob of butter)
150g Parmesan cheese, finely grated
1 teaspoon fresh thyme leaves
Extra virgin olive oil, for drizzling
Salt and freshly ground black pepper

Heat the oil and butter in a heavy-based saucepan. Add the shallots or onion and sweat gently for 5 minutes until soft and translucent but not coloured. Add the rice and stir to fully coat.

Begin adding the hot stock ladle by ladle, stirring all the while, until enough liquid is absorbed that you have a soft creamy dish and the grains retain just a little bite. This should take around 15–20 minutes.

Meanwhile drop the spinach, peas and garlic into a large pan of boiling water. Just as they are about to return to the boil, drain. In a blender, combine them with the cream, half the Parmesan, thyme and plenty of black pepper, till you have a fairly smooth purée. Season to taste.

Stir the purée into the rice. Divide between plates and finish with a few drops of best olive oil and the rest of the Parmesan.

summer-ish food

summer-ish food ... in a rush

watercress, watermelon and feta salad

Combine chunks of watermelon (seeds and skins discarded) and feta with watercress, and dress with olive oil, a squeeze of lemon, and plenty of pepper.

pan-fried fish with mango chilli salsa

Dredge lemon sole fillets on both sides in seasoned flour, and pan-fry in foaming butter until golden and crispy and just cooked through (about 3 minutes on each side). Finely chop a fresh chilli, ½ red onion and mix with cubed fresh mango and a squeeze of lime.

spaghetti with lemon and basil

Beat together one part lemon juice and two parts extra virgin olive oil (or basil oil if you have it). Add enough finely grated Parmesan to turn it into a creamy, emulsified sauce, and toss with al dente pasta. Tear over fresh basil leaves if you have some to hand, and a good grinding of salt and fresh pepper.

crab and fennel salad

Mix together white and brown meat, with a little good mayonnaise and lemon juice to taste. Top and tail fennel bulbs, and slice very finely lengthways. Scatter over a bed of soft, mild leaves dressed simply with good olive oil and lemon juice, spooning the crab on top.

beetroot, mozzarella and basil salad

Top and tail beetroot, turn in oil and sea salt, and roast, covered in foil, at 180°C/gas 4 for 45–60 minutes, depending on size. Rub off the skin, slice and lay out as a robust alternative to tomatoes, with mozzarella (or better still, creamy burrata), basil and best olive oil.

grilled mackerel with bay

Slip a bay leaf – preferably fresh – into the cavity of a gutted fish. Make two slashes diagonally in the skin to allow it to swell and put under a hot grill for 3–4 minutes on each side.

everyone yearns for summer. A time of ease, when you get to snatch tiny moments of holiday from the most banal of situations, graze through the day and drink rosé like water. Listen hard and across the land you'll hear the scraping of office chairs being pushed back in the rush to get outside. It's a hopeful time.

Like everything else, we eat differently during summer months. With our patchy weather, a barbecue summer is as much a state of mind as a reality, and what you put on your plate is one of the best ways of getting it. This is not the time to spend hours dreaming over a slow-roast joint. Instead, it's about taking the best of the season and treating it lightly and simply – fresh flavours, bright colours, quick results.

The food in this chapter reflects this spirit. It is packed with the distinctive colours and young flavours of the season: mild juicy garlic, fresh green herbs, postbox-red tomatoes, dappled pink crab. Since summer eating is as much about picking and grazing as it is complete meals, most of the dishes will happily slot into a larger spread.

You may never be sure whether you'll need sunglasses or a parka every time you step out of the door, but with these recipes you can always conjure up a little piece of summer on your plate.

three bold barbecues

sticky ribs — These ribs are deliciously sticky, the rich, sweet flavours of the marinade bringing out the best in the meat. If the ribs are very large, get your butcher to saw them in half across the bone so they are stubby, and then cut them into three or four rib sections.

feeds 4

1kg rack pork ribs
Zingy slaw (p.271), to serve

for the marinade:
2 large garlic cloves, peeled
1 teaspoon salt
1 tablespoon soft brown sugar
1 tablespoon English mustard

100g tomato ketchup
2 tablespoons pomegranate molasses
2 tablespoons cider vinegar
Juice of ½ lemon
2 tablespoons Worcestershire sauce
3 tablespoons dark soy sauce
1 tablespoon clear honey or agave nectar

To prepare the marinade, pound the garlic with the salt until it forms a paste, and mix well with the rest of the marinade ingredients.

Put the ribs in a medium roasting tin – they should fit snugly. Slather over the marinade, turning and coating very thoroughly. Cover and place in the fridge to marinate for at least a few hours.

Prepare the barbecue for cooking.

An hour before you're ready to cook, take the meat out of the fridge and allow it to come back to room temperature. Wipe off any excess marinade, carefully reserving it in the dish.

Barbecue the ribs for about 12–15 minutes, turning often, until they are deep golden and chewy.

Return the ribs to the tin and sit the tin on the barbecue. Add 4 tablespoons of water and bring to a boil, turning the ribs from time to time. After a few minutes, the sauce should reduce and become sticky. Cut into single ribs and eat immediately, accompanied by zingy slaw.

chicken under a brick – This is a fantastic way of cooking a whole chicken in half the time it takes to roast, and is perfect with any combination of salads that you can cobble together on a summer evening, particularly the Lentil and herb salad on p.271. Ask the butcher to spatchcock the chicken for you if you can, otherwise follow the instructions below.

You will need a couple of foil-covered bricks or a flameproof casserole with a litre or two of water in it to act as an alternative weight.

feeds 4

1.3kg chicken

for the marinade:
2 tablespoons chopped fresh oregano leaves
Pinch dried chilli flakes
2 garlic cloves, finely chopped

1 teaspoon olive oil
Grated zest and juice of ½ unwaxed lemon
Vegetable oil, for rubbing
Salt and freshly ground black pepper

Prepare the barbecue for cooking.

To spatchcock the chicken, place it on its breast with the tail nearest to you, and use poultry shears or a sharp pair of kitchen scissors to cut down both sides of the backbone and remove it completely. Give it a whack with the heel of your hand to flatten it (a meat mallet would be the right tool here if you have one).

Place the oregano, chilli flakes, garlic, olive oil and lemon zest and juice in a small bowl and stir well to combine. Push half this mixture under the skin of the breast as evenly as you can, and the rest under the skin of the legs and thighs. Rub generously with the vegetable oil, and scrunch over salt and a good scramble of pepper. If you have time, set the chicken aside to marinate.

Wait until the heat of the barbecue has subsided a little. Put the chicken on the barbecue, breast-side down, and cover with the foil-covered bricks or flameproof casserole. Cook, without moving, until the skin is golden and crisp, about 10–12 minutes. Remove the weight, turn over and weight again. Cook for 15–20 minutes until the juices run clear when you pierce the thigh.

Allow the chicken to rest for 10–15 minutes before serving. It is easier to cut the chicken into joints with scissors or a cleaver rather than try to carve the meat off.

spiced butterflied leg of lamb with cucumber raita

Butterflied leg of lamb – boned, and splayed out – makes a perfect cut for a barbecue. It's tricky to do at home so ask the butcher to do it for you.

feeds 4

Seeds from 12 cardamom
  pods
10 black peppercorns
3 whole allspice
2 cloves
1½ teaspoons cumin seeds
1 teaspoon coriander seeds
1 tablespoon coarse sea salt

1 teaspoon ground
  cinnamon
2 tablespoons sweet
  paprika
2 tablespoons grated fresh
  root ginger
1 leg of lamb, about 1.3kg,
  boned and butterflied

Flatbreads (p.245) or
  pitta bread, to serve

for the raita:
½ cucumber, grated
300g natural yoghurt
Pinch ground cumin
Salt

First grind the spices and salt, either in a spice grinder or pepper mill or using a pestle and mortar. Mix them with the cinnamon, sweet paprika and ginger and rub all over your lamb, working into all the crevices. Place the lamb in a lidded airtight container or a large plastic food bag and set aside in the fridge for 24 hours to marinate.

Prepare the barbecue for cooking. Remove the meat from the fridge and allow it to come back to room temperature before cooking.

When the barbecue is ready, put the meat on. Cook for 10–12 minutes on one side, not moving the meat until you are ready to turn it over.

Carefully turn the lamb over and cook for a further 10–12 minutes. It's worth making a cut into the plumpest part of the meat after 5 minutes to check how it's doing. As the thickness of the meat is not uniform, neither will the cooking be, which works well with lamb, as some people like it more cooked than others.

Meanwhile, make the raita. Place the cucumber in a colander and salt generously. Allow to sit for 30 minutes on a tray to catch the water. Discard that water, rinse the cucumber and pat dry, then mix with the yoghurt and cumin.

When the meat is cooked to your liking, allow it to rest for 15 minutes. Slice the lamb and serve with flatbreads or toasted pitta bread and the raita.

three glamorous salads

courgette, fresh pea and ricotta salad — If you come
across any pea shoots (they are becoming more widely available at supermarkets)
they would make a wonderful addition here. This salad should be eaten fairly
soon after it is made or it will shrivel.

feeds 4 as a starter or part of a spread

1 unwaxed lemon
4 baby courgettes
100g fresh podded peas
200g ricotta cheese
Extra virgin olive oil, for drizzling
Freshly ground black pepper

Carefully pare the zest from the lemon, avoiding any white pith, and cut it into
thin strips. Cut the lemon in half and set aside.

Top and tail the courgettes and cut them into ribbons – you can do this carefully
with a vegetable peeler, or easily with a mandolin. Lay the courgette ribbons
in a dish with the peas (and pea shoots if you have any). Dot over the ricotta,
being careful to drain off any excess water. Scatter with the strips of lemon zest,
grind over some black pepper, squeeze over lemon juice and drizzle with extra
virgin olive oil.

club 55 tomato salad

club 55 tomato salad – This salad originates from Club 55, St-Tropez's famous beach club. It makes the best of ripe summer tomatoes, which are given a totally different sparkle by the thick tangy dressing and fresh mint.

feeds 4 for a starter or side or 2 for a simple lunch with crusty bread

4 beefsteak or large heritage tomatoes
250g goats' cheese log
3 tablespoons chopped fresh mint

for the dressing:
100ml sunflower or vegetable oil
50ml extra virgin olive oil
1 tablespoon Dijon mustard
1 tablespoon white wine vinegar
Salt and freshly ground black pepper

Slice the tomatoes thickly and lay out, overlapping, on a platter. Remove the rind of the goats' cheese and roughly crumble over the top.

Beat together (or even better, blend) the dressing ingredients with a pinch of salt until emulsified. Pour over the top, scatter over the mint and grind over some fresh black pepper.

lentil, tenderstem broccoli and goats' cheese salad

This salad is substantial enough to eat as the main dish in a larger spread, with some crusty bread. It is fine to use ready-cooked, vacuum-packed lentils. You could happily replace the broccoli with French beans, too.

feeds 4 for a starter or 2 for lunch

for the salad:
250g cooked Puy lentils or 125g
  uncooked Puy lentils plus vegetable
  stock for cooking
200g tenderstem or purple sprouting
  broccoli
1 heaped tablespoon chopped flat-leaf
  parsley
1 heaped tablespoon chopped fresh mint
2 spring onions, sliced
100g goats' cheese log

for the dressing:
3 tablespoons olive oil
Juice of ½ lemon
1 tablespoon Dijon mustard
1 heaped tablespoon crème fraîche
Salt and freshly ground black pepper

If you are starting with uncooked lentils, simmer them in the vegetable stock until just tender, about 25–30 minutes. Drain.

Meanwhile, chop the very bottom of the broccoli stems off and discard. Cut the remaining broccoli into 5cm batons. Steam or blanch for a couple of minutes in boiling water till just al dente, plunge into cold water then drain.

Mix the broccoli with the cooked lentils, herbs and spring onions.

Beat together the dressing ingredients, seasoning to taste, and adding a little water to thin if it becomes too thick and sticky. Carefully toss together with the salad.

Finally, pare off the cheese rind and crumble over the top of the salad.

three summer fish

baked sea trout with hazelnuts and samphire

This is a wonderful treat for supper and virtually no effort to make. The salty samphire will wilt and discolour but still taste fantastic, melding beautifully with the buttery hazelnuts to perfectly offset the fish.

feeds 4

1 sea trout, approximately 1.2kg, cleaned
  and gutted, head on
50g butter
4 tablespoons chopped hazelnuts
150g samphire
Buttered new potatoes with mint, to serve

Preheat the oven to 180°C/gas 4.

Lay out a square of foil, large enough to wrap and secure around the fish. Place the fish on the foil, on a baking tray.

Melt the butter in a pan and add the hazelnuts. Gently fry for a few minutes until they begin to colour, then toss with the samphire. Push the samphire mixture into the fish cavity.

Wrap the fish in the foil, to form a sealed package, and bake for 15–20 minutes until the flesh is just opaque and lifts easily from the bone. When ready, remove the fish from the oven, and open the package, being careful not to lose any liquid.

Lift the fillet off the bone in four large pieces, and transfer onto plates, spooning the samphire, nuts and juices over the fish. Serve with buttered new potatoes scattered with mint.

pan-roast pollack with tomatoes, anchovies and capers

— Pan roasting (starting off on the hob and finishing in the oven) is an excellent cooking method for thick-cut fish or meat, as it allows the outside to colour and crisp up whilst retaining a juicy interior. Here, the summery sauce – almost a salsa – makes the flavour of the fish soar.

feeds 4

Olive oil, for frying
4 x 200g thick-cut pollack fillets,
    or other firm white fish fillets
New potatoes, to serve

for the sauce:
2 large tomatoes
1 tablespoon capers in brine, rinsed,
    drained and chopped
4 anchovy fillets in olive oil, drained
6 tablespoons olive oil
2 garlic cloves, very finely sliced
Salt and freshly ground black pepper

Preheat the oven to 180°C/gas 4.

Prick the tomatoes a few times with a sharp knife and place them in a bowl of just-boiled water. After a couple of minutes the skins will peel back. Remove the skins completely. Cut the tomatoes in half, discard the seeds and membranes, and finely chop the flesh.

Place all the sauce ingredients with plenty of seasoning in a small pan and gently heat them together until the anchovy has disintegrated and the garlic is soft but not coloured, about 3–4 minutes. Remove from the heat and transfer to a bowl to prevent further cooking.

Add a little olive oil to an ovenproof frying pan, and put over a high heat. Place the fish, skin-side down, in the pan and sear until the skin is golden and crispy, about 3–4 minutes. Turn over and do the same underneath, then transfer to the oven until the fish is just cooked through, about another 3–4 minutes. The fish will be cooked when the flesh turns opaque and flakes easily.

Serve with the sauce on top or on the side and with new potatoes.

fennel-stuffed bream on new potatoes – This is a
lovely all-in-one treatment for fish that is quick to bang in the oven and
breathtakingly easy.

feeds 4

500g waxy new potatoes, eg
    Pink Fir Apple or Charlotte
6 sprigs rosemary
1 red onion
2 fennel bulbs
2 sea bream, approximately 400g
    each, scaled and gutted

2 lemons
100ml vegetable stock
Splash of Pernod (optional)
Olive oil, for drizzling
Salt and freshly ground black pepper
Salsa verde (p.273) and Good old green
    salad (p.271), to serve

Preheat the oven to 180°C/gas 4.

Slice the potatoes lengthways to the thickness of a pound coin and spread over
the base of a roasting tin. Tuck in the rosemary, season well and place in the oven.

Thinly slice the onion and fennel lengthways. Divide between the cavities of
both fish. Slice one lemon and lay the slices inside, too (save the other lemon
to cut into wedges).

After the potatoes have been cooking for 10 minutes carefully lay the fish on
top. Pour the stock over the fish, add a splash of Pernod, if using, and finish with
a coat of olive oil and plenty of salt and pepper.

Roast for 20 minutes until the fish is just opaque, the liquid has evaporated, and
the potatoes are golden and tender. Eat with a wedge of lemon, salsa verde and
a green salad.

three seasonal pastas

courgette linguine – This is a high-season dish, bringing out the best in the courgettes by melting them in olive oil until completely tender. It calls for top-notch extra virgin olive oil.

feeds 4

5 medium courgettes
400g linguine
3 tablespoons extra virgin olive oil
4 small or 2 medium garlic cloves,
  finely chopped

2 tablespoons chopped fresh mint
Salt and freshly ground black pepper
Grated Parmesan cheese, to serve

First grate the courgettes on the coarse side of a box grater. If you have time, put into a colander or sieve and shake over plenty of salt. Set aside to drain for 20 minutes. Rinse the grated courgettes in fresh water and pat dry.

Cook the pasta in plenty of well-salted boiling water according to the packet instructions, until al dente.

Over a high heat, warm the olive oil in a large sauté or frying pan. Add the courgettes, and fry for a couple of minutes to allow the water to evaporate, then turn the heat down before they start to colour. Shake and turn, frying gently for a further 7–10 minutes, then add the garlic, and cook for 1 minute.

When the spaghetti is al dente, drain and toss with the courgettes. Scatter with the mint, grind over black pepper and be generous with the Parmesan.

pasta with ricotta, aubergine and pine nuts

This is a richly delectable bowl of pasta, perfect for a late-summer evening when the vegetables still have the warmth of the sun in them, but the air has the beginnings of a nip in it.

feeds 4

1 aubergine, topped, tailed and diced
  into 2cm cubes
Olive oil, for roasting
100g pine nuts
2 large fresh tomatoes
400g tacconelli or other short pasta,
  like penne

150g ricotta
60g wild rocket, any large stems removed
Freshly ground black pepper
Parmesan cheese and extra virgin
  olive oil, to serve

Preheat the oven to 230°C/gas 8.

Toss the aubergine in olive oil, spread out in a roasting tin and roast, turning from time to time, until golden all over, about 15–20 minutes.

Meanwhile, in a dry frying pan, toast the pine nuts over a medium heat, tossing, until golden but not burnt – be careful, they can burn quickly. Tip out onto a plate and set aside.

Prick the tomatoes a few times with a sharp knife and place them in a bowl of just-boiled water. After a couple of minutes, when the skins peel back, remove completely and discard. Cut the tomatoes in half, discard the seeds and membranes, and chop the flesh into small pieces.

Cook the pasta in plenty of well-salted boiling water according to the packet instructions, until al dente.

Warm a large serving bowl, and add to it the ricotta, tomato, pine nuts and a couple of tablespoons of the pasta cooking water, and stir to form a cream. Drain the pasta without shaking it too dry and toss with the ricotta mixture, adding the aubergine and rocket. Continue to toss and turn delicately, so that the pasta is well coated and the ingredients are well distributed.

Drizzle with best olive oil and serve with shavings of fresh Parmesan and plenty of black pepper.

spaghetti with herbs – I discovered this last summer when my sister planted for my birthday a generous herb garden in a tub to keep on the balcony. I like a bowl of this to accompany a snacking sort of supper – leftovers of whatever meats and cheeses are in the fridge, or even just a large tomato salad – the Club 55 salad (p.194) would be perfect.

feeds 4

400g spaghetti
1 small garlic clove
4 tablespoons extra virgin olive oil
8 tablespoons finely chopped mixed fresh
   herbs, eg oregano, parsley, mint, chives,
   thyme and tarragon
Sea salt and freshly ground black pepper
Parmesan cheese, to serve

Cook the spaghetti in plenty of well-salted boiling water according to the packet instructions, until perfectly al dente. Drain and reserve 2 tablespoons of the cooking liquor.

Meanwhile, crush the garlic with a pinch of salt to form a paste.

Add the olive oil, garlic paste and herbs to the pasta along with the reserved cooking water and plenty of black pepper, and toss very well over the heat, for about 20 seconds. Serve immediately with a scrunch of sea salt and shavings of fresh Parmesan.

three savoury tarts

simple cherry tomato tart — Ready-made puff pastry is one of the most useful bases if you want to make something elegant in a hurry. This tart brings out the best in the tomatoes and is great as a starter or part of a spread.

feeds 4

500g cherry tomatoes, halved
3 tablespoons extra virgin olive oil
3 tablespoons chopped, mixed fresh herbs, eg oregano, tarragon, mint, thyme
375g ready-rolled all-butter puff pastry, thawed if frozen

Oil, for greasing
1 tablespoon Dijon mustard
3 tablespoons grated Gruyère cheese
2 tablespoons grated Parmesan cheese
1 egg, beaten
Salt and freshly ground black pepper

First, toss the tomatoes with the oil, 2 tablespoons of the herbs, salt and pepper and set aside to marinate for a while.

Preheat the oven to 200°C/gas 6.

Lay the pastry sheet out on a lightly oiled baking sheet and carefully score a rectangle 1.5cm in from the edges, to half the depth of the pastry.

Spread the mustard over the middle area of the pastry and scatter with the cheeses. Lay the tomatoes cut-side up over the cheeses. Brush the outer marked edges of pastry with the beaten egg.

Bake for 30–35 minutes until the sides have puffed up and are golden and the tomatoes are soft, sweet, and starting to blacken in places.

Finally, scatter with the remaining herbs and allow to cool a little before serving.

smoked haddock, gruyère and leek tart – This is a
delicious tart: the young, sweet leeks balance the smoky undertones of the fish. You can cheat with ready-made all-butter pastry which makes the whole exercise so much less effort.

feeds 4
you will need a 23cm loose-bottomed tart tin

Butter, for greasing
250g ready-made all-butter
  shortcrust pastry
Flour, for rolling
100g baby leeks
15g butter

Pinch saffron threads
250g smoked haddock fillet
4 egg yolks
200ml double cream
30g Gruyère cheese, grated
Freshly ground black pepper

Preheat the oven to 190°C/gas 5. Grease the tin.

Roll out the pastry to the thickness of a pound coin on a floured surface and transfer to the tin, allowing a little to flop over the sides. Use any trimmings to plug gaps up the side. Prick with a fork, lay a sheet of baking parchment over and half fill with baking beans (any dried pulses will do). Bake for 15 minutes, then remove the beans and paper and return to the oven for 10 minutes, until beginning to smell biscuity and turn slightly coloured. Trim off any excess pastry from around the edges with the back of a knife.

Meanwhile, trim the leeks and make a deep cross right through the tender white and pale green part. Slice across 1cm thick so that you end up with little 1cm squares of leek. Heat the butter in a small pan and gently sweat the leeks, adding the saffron, until soft but not coloured, about 7–10 minutes.

Put the haddock into a saucepan and completely cover with water. Bring to the boil then switch off and allow to stand for 5 minutes. Remove the fish and set aside to cool. Break up into chunky flakes, discarding any skin and bones.

Whisk together the egg yolks, cream, half the Gruyère and a sprinkling of black pepper. Arrange the fish and the leeks in the pastry case and pour over the egg and cream mixture, sprinkling the rest of the Gruyère over the top. Place on a baking sheet and cook for 30 minutes, until the top is golden and just springy. Leave to cool slightly – or completely – before serving.

spring onion, herb and goats' cheese tart — This tart

is filled with bright, summer flavours, and makes a perfect lunch with a salad
or two on the side.

feeds 4
you will need a 23cm loose-bottomed tart tin

Butter, for greasing
250g ready-made all-butter
  shortcrust pastry
Flour, for rolling
1 bunch spring onions
3 eggs

150ml double cream
1 small handful of chopped summer herbs,
  eg mint, tarragon, parsley or chervil
100g goats' cheese log
Salt and freshly ground black pepper
Good old green salad (p.271), to serve

Preheat the oven to 190°C/gas 5. Grease the tin.

Roll out the pastry to the thickness of a pound coin on a floured surface and
transfer to the tin, allowing a little to flop over the sides. Use any trimmings to
plug gaps up the side. Prick with a fork, lay a sheet of baking parchment over
and half fill with baking beans (any dried pulses will do). Bake for 15 minutes,
then remove the beans and paper and return to the oven for 10 minutes, until
beginning to smell biscuity and turn slightly coloured. Trim off any excess pastry
from around the edges with the back of a knife.

Meanwhile, trim the spring onions, discarding the roots and the very dark green
stems, then blanch for 30 seconds in boiling salted water. Allow to drain and pat
dry. Cut all but 1 onion into small rounds.

Lightly beat the eggs, cream, herbs, and chopped spring onions together,
crumbling in the goats' cheese. Pour the mixture carefully into the pastry
case and lay the single spring onion on top. Bake for 30 minutes until just
firm and golden.

Allow to cool for a few minutes – or entirely – before eating with salad.

pudding!

pudding! ... in a rush

cheat's ice cream cake

Allow a tub of good ice cream to soften just enough to become stirrable with some effort. Add your favourite chocolate – I like crushed Maltesers or Munchies, or shattered After Eights, and stir through. Line a small loose-bottomed cake tin with clingfilm and spoon in the ice cream mixture. Cover with clingfilm and return to the freezer. When you are ready to eat, turn the cake out onto a plate and dust with sieved cocoa powder.

roasted peaches or plums

Halve and pit your fruit and lay cut-side up in a roasting tray. Sprinkle with a little caster sugar (and Marsala, sherry or sweet wine if you have some). Roast at 180°C/gas 4 for 25 minutes or until tender, and eat with mascarpone or cream beaten with a couple of tablespoons of the booze if you are using it.

greek yoghurt with rosewater, honey, pistachios and sultanas

Stir a teaspoon of rosewater through a tub of Greek yoghurt. Generously drizzle with good clear honey and scatter with pistachios and large sultanas.

quick raspberry tart

Make (or buy) a large, cooked sweet pastry case, or several small ones. Enrich mascarpone by beating in a little very fresh egg yolk and sugar and spread over the bottom. Arrange fresh raspberries in circles.

baked figs with honey and marsala

Stand the fruit on foil. Make a cross through the top of the figs to half way down and squeeze to open. Spoon in equal amounts of clear honey and Marsala and a little chopped fresh thyme if you like. Wrap up into a parcel and bake for 10 minutes at 180°C/gas 4 until warm and soft. Open the package for the last 5 minutes to let the juices reduce. Serve as they are, or with crème fraîche or fresh goats' cheese.

strawberries in elderflower cordial

Macerate strawberries in elderflower cordial. Serve with a little sugar and cream or ice cream.

the world is divided into those for whom pudding is something extra, a treat for special occasions, and those for whom it is an integral part of the meal. You can spot this species a mile off – they are the ones who, in restaurants, look at the dessert section of the menu before deciding what they are going to order.

Homemade puddings have somehow gone out of fashion. Without wanting to come over all sentimental, it feels like a whole generation is in danger of growing up without knowing the joys of a crumble, its steaming fruit slipping out from underneath a collapsing golden topping, or a wobbling jelly, set from the burgundy juices of very ripe plums. Pudding is the one area of traditional English cookery that has always held its head high.

Not to say that all puddings should be old-fashioned, nor that the ones in this chapter are. Some take familiar recipes and find a new (and often simpler) way in, others are just straightforward classics that need not be messed with. What they all have in common is that they take the best ingredients and celebrate them.

A note about the serving sizes in this chapter – with pudding, it's never more than a suggestion. While some will resist more than a sliver, others are guaranteed to come back for more. So while each recipe is written to feed four, this can only ever be the loosest of guides.

Complicated desserts should be saved for restaurants, of that there's no question. But there will always be room at the kitchen table for dishes that smell like heaven, taste even better, and are met with coos of pleasure. You might regret eating too much pudding, but you'll never regret having made it.

simple pear custard tart – This tart is sophisticated at the same time as being blindingly easy. Look for pears that are firm enough not to collapse, whilst ripe enough to be sweet and giving.

feeds 4
you will need a 20cm loose-bottomed tart tin

Butter, for greasing
375g ready-made, ready-rolled all-butter
  sweet or plain shortcrust pastry
3 fairly ripe but firm pears, eg Comice
200ml double cream
2 egg yolks
2 tablespoons vanilla or caster sugar

Preheat the oven to 190°C/gas 5. Lightly grease the tin.

Lay the pastry over the tin, allowing a little to flop over the edges (it often shrinks with baking). Prick with a fork all over and lay in a sheet of baking parchment. Half fill with baking beans (any dried pulses will do) and bake for 15 minutes. Remove the beans (you can use them again and again) and the paper and return to the oven for 10 minutes. When smelling biscuity and starting to turn golden, remove the pastry and set aside – you can do this in advance if you like.

Meanwhile, peel, core and carefully slice the pears, then arrange them in the pastry case as artfully as you can. Place the pastry case on a baking tray. Beat the cream with the egg yolks and sugar and pour over the pears. Return to the oven and bake for 45–50 minutes, until the filling has just set and is tinged with gold. If it begins to colour too fast, loosely cover with foil. Allow to cool to room temperature, and gently chip off any excess pastry with the back of a large knife before serving.

apple crumble — I've never met anyone who turns down apple crumble. You can add whatever you like to make it more seasonal – a couple of spoonfuls of elderflower cordial in the summer, a handful of blackberries in the autumn, some chunks of rhubarb in spring.

feeds 4

Juice of ½ lemon
3 cooking apples, peeled, cored and sliced
75g self-raising flour
75g rolled porridge oats
130g butter, cubed
1 heaped tablespoon granulated sugar
1 heaped tablespoon demerara sugar

Preheat the oven to 180°C/gas 4.

Toss the lemon juice through the apples as soon as they are sliced and lay them in the bottom of a 23cm round baking dish.

Place the remaining ingredients in a large mixing bowl and rub together until you have a breadcrumb consistency. Scatter the crumbs over the apples and bake for 30–40 minutes, until golden on top, with the apples bubbling out at the sides.

seville orange posset — Posset, a thickened cream cut with tangy citrus, is a delicious end to any supper. You can substitute lemons when Seville oranges are not in season. Serve in pretty glasses, with shortbread or cantucci.

feeds 4

2 Seville oranges
500ml double cream
150g caster sugar
Shortbread or cantucci, to serve

Grate the zest from ½ of one of the oranges. Squeeze the juice from both oranges (there is relatively little juice in Seville oranges).

Bring the cream and the sugar to the boil in a small pan and stir until the sugar has completely dissolved. Remove from the heat and whisk in the orange juice and zest.

Pour into glasses from a height (this helps the posset to cool and adds air), then allow to cool and refrigerate overnight before eating.

Delicious with shortbread or cantucci.

eastern trifle – This is a fabulously scented trifle which is simplified by cutting out the jelly and replacing traditional custard with a light, eggy mascarpone cream. Unless it is the season for very good fruit, you would be better off using top-quality compote and tinned varieties rather than fresh fruit. If you cannot find nibbed pistachios, bash peeled, unsalted pistachios in a pestle and mortar instead.

feeds 4

1 Earl Grey teabag
1 cup boiling water
12 sponge fingers
200g raspberries or
  raspberry compote
200g mascarpone
2 eggs, separated

1 tablespoon caster sugar
1 tablespoon orange blossom water
2 peaches, fresh or tinned in light syrup,
  or 2 very ripe mangoes
150ml whipping cream
30g nibbed pistachios or flaked almonds

Place the teabag in a cup and cover with boiling water. Leave to infuse for a couple of minutes and then remove the teabag. Set the cup of tea aside to cool for 15 minutes.

Lay a couple of layers of sponge fingers into the bottom of a glass serving dish and cover them with just enough tea for them to soak it up completely. Scatter over a layer of raspberries.

To make the custardy cream, beat together the mascarpone, egg yolks, sugar and orange blossom water. In a separate bowl, beat the egg whites into soft peaks, then fold into the custard with a metal spoon. Spoon the custard over the raspberries in the dish.

Slice the peaches or mangoes and add them in a layer over the custard cream. Beat the whipping cream until it forms very soft peaks and smear over the fruit. Cover and refrigerate.

When you are ready to eat, scatter over the pistachios or almonds.

chocolate and hazelnut meringue brownie cake

This is deliciously light, chewy and chocolatey, without being sickly and rich. The spiced hot chocolate can be sipped alongside or used as a dip.

feeds 4

you will need a 20cm loose-bottomed tart tin

for the cake:

Butter, for greasing

100g 70% cocoa solids dark chocolate, broken into pieces

150g caster sugar

3 eggs, separated

1 teaspoon vanilla extract

40g finely ground hazelnuts

40g whole hazelnuts

Icing sugar, for dusting

for the hot chocolate:

300ml double cream

1 cinnamon stick

1 dried chilli, broken in half

100g 70% cocoa solids dark chocolate, broken into pieces

Preheat the oven to 180°C/gas 4. Grease the tin.

Place the chocolate pieces, for the brownies, in a large heatproof mixing bowl and set it over (not in) a pan of simmering water. Stir until the chocolate melts. Add 100g of the caster sugar and stir until it dissolves – it may not completely, but that's fine. Set aside to cool for 10 minutes or so.

Meanwhile, in another, very clean, bowl, beat the egg whites until they form soft peaks, adding the remaining sugar in thirds, so that you have a glossy meringue mixture, and set aside.

Now add the egg yolks and vanilla extract to the melted chocolate and beat in well with an electric mixer. Fold in the ground and whole hazelnuts, then the egg whites, a spoonful at a time. Scrape into the cake tin and bake for 20 minutes – the cake will feel firm and look a little cracked on the top.

Leave to cool for at least 15 minutes.

Meanwhile, make the hot chocolate. Put the cream into a saucepan with the cinnamon and chilli and bring just to the boil. Add the chocolate, stirring until smooth and the chocolate has completely melted. Remove the cinnamon and chilli.

Carefully remove the cake from the tin. Dust with icing sugar and cut into thin wedges. Serve wedges of cake, with the hot chocolate served alongside in espresso cups.

plum and sauternes jelly — This jelly looks like a jewel and has

a wonderfully delicate flavour and texture. Remember it will need at least four hours to set, or even better, overnight.

feeds 4
you will need a 500ml jelly mould or glass bowl

125g caster sugar	Groundnut oil or other flavourless oil,
500g plums	for greasing
5 leaves gelatine	Thick cream or ice cream and thin
100ml Sauternes	almond biscuits, to serve

Heat 250ml water and the sugar together in a medium pan over a low heat, stirring until the sugar has dissolved. Add the whole plums, cover and turn the heat right down. Poach the fruit gently for 15–20 minutes then switch off the heat and allow to cool so the flavours can continue to develop.

Strain the plums through a sieve and measure out 400ml of the poaching liquid, then set aside. Reserve the remaining liquid and press the very soft plums through a sieve into this liquid, to make a compote, then refrigerate.

To make the jelly, soak the gelatine leaves in a large jug of cold water for 5 minutes until completely floppy.

Reheat 100ml of the poaching liquid until it is just about to boil. Drain the gelatine, place in a bowl, then pour the hot liquid over it, stirring until the gelatine dissolves completely. Add the further 300ml of the poaching liquid, continuing to stir, and then add the Sauternes.

Very sparingly wipe the mould or bowl with the oil. Pour the jelly into the mould or bowl, cover and leave in the fridge to set for at least four hours.

Remove the compote from the fridge about an hour before serving to allow it to come to room temperature. To turn the jelly out, briefly dip the mould or bowl in a large bowl of very hot water, place a plate on top and then quickly invert the mould or bowl, holding on tight to the plate, so that the jelly slides onto the plate. Serve with the compote, very good, thick cream or ice cream and thin almond biscuits.

daisy's molten chocolate puds

daisy's molten chocolate puds — These delicious little puddings always come out perfectly gooey on the inside. My friend Daisy's tip is to turn them out when the top still looks a bit damp, rather than totally cooked through. While the timing is precise, the method is not challenging.

feeds 4
you will need 4 x 6cm aluminium baking rings (from good cookshops)
or 4 individual ramekins or metal pudding basins

125g 70% cocoa solids dark
  chocolate, broken into pieces
110g butter, cubed
50g plain flour, sifted

3 eggs
150g caster sugar
Crème fraîche or double cream, to serve

Preheat the oven to 190°C/gas 5. Line a baking tray with baking parchment. Put the rings on the baking tray and line each one with a collar of greaseproof paper that stands a bit higher than the ring.

Place the chocolate pieces and half the butter in a heatproof mixing bowl and set it over (not in) a pan of simmering water until it melts. Once melted, add the remaining butter so it melts too but also brings down the temperature of the mix. Next stir in the flour.

Beat the eggs and sugar together in a large mixing bowl, either using a hand-held electric mixer or by hand. If doing it by hand use big movements – the aim is to get lots of air into it.

Carefully fold the chocolate mixture into the egg mixture. Spoon it evenly into the prepared rings and refrigerate until ready to cook.

Bake for 9–10 minutes from room temperature, or 11–12 from the fridge. When perfect, they will still look damp on top. Carefully slip off the rings and peel off the paper. Serve immediately with crème fraîche or double cream.

filo fruit parcel – This pudding is a very easy way of presenting something that looks impressive. This version of it is a classic autumnal combination, but all the soft summer fruit – peaches, nectarines, berries – would work very well, too.

feeds 4

2 medium cooking apples, peeled, cored and thinly sliced
400g frozen or fresh blackberries
50ml apple juice

2–3 tablespoons granulated sugar
4 sheets filo pastry
75g butter, melted
Icing sugar and double cream, to serve

Preheat the oven to 180°C/gas 4.

Place the apple slices, blackberries, apple juice and sugar (to taste) in a medium pan and stew gently for a few minutes, until just giving. Allow to cool a little.

Lay 2 filo sheets out on 2 baking sheets and brush with melted butter. Lay another on top of each at a different angle, again brush with butter.

Remove the fruit from the pan with a slotted spoon, leaving behind most of the juice (reserve this). Divide the fruit equally between the centres of the 2 pastries. Gather the sides up and twist together at the top, to form 2 moneybags. Bake for 15–20 minutes until the pastry is golden and crisp.

Transfer the reserved juices to a jug. Dust the cooked pastries with icing sugar and put each between two people, to share. Serve with cream and the juices.

scented eton mess — This is an unbeatable summer pudding.
I like to include a sprinkling of rosewater, which really brings out the fragrance of the strawberries.

feeds 4

250g ripe strawberries
1 tablespoon rosewater
2 tablespoons caster sugar
200ml whipping cream

4 individual meringue nests or
1 large meringue base
Freshly ground black pepper

Wash, hull, and cut the strawberries into smallish pieces. Sprinkle with the rosewater, sugar and a scant turn of black pepper and set aside to macerate for at least 15 minutes, longer if possible.

Whip the cream until it forms soft peaks.

Crush half the strawberries with a fork. Break up the meringues.

Fold the cream, strawberries and meringues together, so that everything is streaked pale pink. Divide between four glasses to serve.

peach and blueberry sponge pudding

– This glorious fruit-stained summer sponge is also excellent with apples in the winter instead of peaches and blueberries. Make sure your dish is small enough (I use a 20cm round one) so that the sponge towers up over the edges, like a big blowsy hat.

feeds 4

Butter, for greasing
3 fresh or good-quality bottled peaches, peeled and sliced
200g fresh or frozen blueberries
Juice of ½ lemon
1 teaspoon cornflour, sifted
Crème fraîche or double cream, to serve

for the sponge:
150g butter, softened
100g caster sugar
2 eggs
150g self-raising flour, sifted
75–100ml buttermilk

Preheat the oven to 180°C/gas 4. Grease an ovenproof dish.

Put the peaches, blueberries, lemon juice and cornflour into the dish and stir them together.

To make the sponge, place the butter and sugar in a large bowl and beat until pale and fluffy. Incorporate the eggs one at a time, beating thoroughly in between. Carefully fold in the flour. Add the buttermilk to thin the mixture until it has a soft, dropping consistency.

Spread the mixture over the fruit and bake for 20 minutes until the top is turning golden and the sponge is cooked just through.

Serve with crème fraîche or double cream.

sweet fennel tarte tatin – This is an unusual take on a classic – the fennel turns soft and sweet and deliciously caramelised during cooking.

feeds 4
you will need a 20cm ovenproof frying pan

2 fennel bulbs
3 eating apples
100g butter
120g caster sugar
1 teaspoon fennel seeds
Flour, for dusting

250g ready-made, ready-rolled all-butter
   puff pastry, thawed if frozen
1 egg, lightly beaten
1 teaspoon granulated sugar
Vanilla ice cream, to serve

Trim each fennel at the top and slice a thin layer off the bottom. Cut lengthways into 8 wedges, so that they remain attached at the root. Bring a large pan of water to a rolling boil and blanch the fennel for 1 minute, then drain. Peel and core the apples and cut each into 8 wedges.

Meanwhile, heat the butter and sugar together in a large frying pan until the butter has melted and the sugar dissolved. Add the fennel seeds, blanched fennel and apple. If they are not starting to colour after 10 minutes, drain off the caramel sauce and reserve, then return them to the pan and fry on all sides till golden.

Preheat the oven to 220°C/gas 7.

Lay out the pastry on a floured surface and cut it into a 26cm circle.

Add the caramel to a 20cm ovenproof frying pan and carefully pack the apple and fennel as tightly as possible into the pan. Warm on the hob until starting to bubble, then switch off the heat. Lay over the pastry circle, and turn the edges back so they come back up the sides of the pan. Brush with the beaten egg and scatter with the granulated sugar. Prick the top a couple of times with a fork, and transfer to the oven for 35–40 minutes. After 10 minutes, reduce the temperature to 200°C/gas 6.

When golden on top, remove from the oven and allow to cool in the pan for 5 minutes. Place an inverted plate over the top of the pan, and with one movement, turn both over together, so the tart comes out the right side up on the plate. Scrape over any remaining caramel sauce, and serve warm with vanilla ice cream.

three fruit compotes

susie brooke's cherry compote — Susie is my friend Arabee's mother. She has a beautiful morello cherry tree in her garden and goes into battle with the birds to harvest them every July. She swears this perfect compote is best eaten with chocolate ice cream.

If you can't find morello cherries, which are naturally sour, you'll need to reduce the volume of sugar in the syrup by half.

feeds 4

500g ripe morello cherries
100g caster sugar or fructose
2 tablespoons cherry brandy (optional)

First, pit your cherries – that's the only demanding bit. A cherry (or olive) pitter will help no end.

Put them into a medium pan with 100ml water and bring to the boil. Cook for 15 minutes. Add the sugar, and brandy if you are using it, and, once the sugar has dissolved, reduce to a simmer, and cook until tender and glossy, about another 15 minutes.

If you have too much juice and it is not syrupy enough, remove the cherries with a slotted spoon, and boil the juice to reduce. Return the cherries, allow to cool, and serve with chocolate ice cream.

spiced apple, pear and quince compote – This

autumnal compote has all the warming spices that you look to as the year begins to turn. You could make it as well with any of the fruit alone, as in combination. Serve warm, with vanilla ice cream and shortbread or cantucci.

feeds 4

75g granulated sugar or fructose	2 long strips of orange zest
1 cinnamon stick	1 apple, peeled, cored and sliced
1 star anise	1 pear, peeled, cored and sliced
1 clove	1 quince, peeled, cored and sliced

Place the sugar, spices, orange zest and 150ml water in a pan, bring to the boil, and stir until the sugar dissolves.

Add the fruit, reduce the heat to a mere blip, and cook for 15 minutes until tender. If the liquid is not syrupy enough, set the fruit aside and boil to reduce. Eat warm with ice cream or cool and keep in the fridge for up to a week.

rhubarb, pernod and vanilla compote – This is a perky

winter compote that is best made with the very early, bright pink stems of forced rhubarb that begin to appear in February. Excellent for breakfast with granola and Greek yoghurt.

feeds 4

1 vanilla pod, split lengthways	400g rhubarb, topped, tailed
75g granulated sugar or fructose	and chopped into 5cm pieces
Splash of Pernod (optional)	

Place the vanilla, sugar and Pernod, if using, in a pan with 100ml water. Bring to the boil, stirring to dissolve the sugar.

Reduce the heat, add the fruit and cook for 5–7 minutes until tender but not falling apart. Set aside to cool and keep in the fridge for up to a week.

rose truffles — Truffles are not pudding as such, but often exactly what you want to finish a big dinner with, and making your own seems special whilst being at the same time straightforward.

You can flavour them with whatever takes your fancy instead of the rosewater: try mixed Christmas spices with a pinch of chilli, finely chopped fresh mint or sieved raspberry jam – or of course just leave them plain, too.

makes approximately 50
you will need a 23cm square baking tin

400g 70% cocoa solids dark chocolate
15g unsalted butter
200ml double cream
2 tablespoons rose jam (from Middle
    Eastern shops) or sieved apricot jam

2 tablespoons rosewater
50g cocoa powder, sieved

Line the baking tin with clingfilm. Place a heatproof bowl over a pan of boiling water, making sure that the bowl does not touch the water.

Break the chocolate into the bowl and stir until completely melted, add the butter, stir through, then remove from heat. Stir in the cream, jam and rosewater, then pour into the lined baking tray. Cover and allow to set in the fridge for a couple of hours.

When set, turn the mixture out onto a baking-parchment-lined board and cut into cubes. Put the cocoa into a plastic bag, and add the truffles, a few at a time, shaking around to coat.

The truffles will keep, in an airtight lidded container, for a few days in the fridge, or any extras can be stored in the freezer (they make a delicious frozen snack).

everyday baking

everyday baking ... in a rush

pesto bread

Cut a baguette into slices, but still joined at the bottom, as you would for garlic bread. Spread good pesto on both sides of each slice, wrap in foil, and put in a hot oven for 10 minutes until crusty and fragrant.

homemade sausage rolls

Slip the best sausages you can find out of their skins and microwave on full for a couple of minutes to get them started. Roll up in ready-rolled all-butter puff pastry, seal the edges with a little beaten egg and press together with the tines of a fork. Brush the top with beaten egg and bake in a hot oven (220°C/gas 7) for 20 minutes until the pastry is puffed up and golden and the sausages cooked through.

cereal bars

Warm a tin of condensed milk in a large pan, and stir in enough good-quality, low-sugar muesli until you have a heavy, sticky mass. Oil a large baking tin and spread out the mixture to 1cm deep. Bake in the oven at 140°C/gas 1 for one hour, allow to cool, then cut into bars and store in an airtight container.

rosemary arab breads

Tear up pitta breads (or better still Mediterranean wraps) into large-ish, rough triangles. Drizzle generously with olive oil and scatter with flaky salt and fresh rosemary. Bake in a very hot oven for 10 minutes, turning over half way, until golden and crunchy. Fantastic with dips of all kinds, or just to crunch on.

jam tarts

Oil a cupcake tray and cut circles of all-butter puff pastry to fit. Fill with good-quality jam – I prefer less likely ones such as rose or bitter marmalade. Brush the edges with egg wash, dust with granulated sugar, and bake in a pre-heated oven at 220°C/gas 7 for 20 minutes. Allow to cool before removing.

it has always seemed to me that baking is a skill quite apart from cooking. There are rules to follow, and instructions to carry out. It involves precision, and tidiness, and organisation. It's the kind of cooking that either sends you into a frenzy of panic or allows you to heave a great sigh of relief.

Twist and turn as you might, at some point, your baking years will be upon you. For practical reasons: the loaf of bread when all the shops are shut, or scones, still warm, for tea. There will always be cupcakes to make for children's parties, or flatbread to whip up as impromptu pizza bases when nothing else will do. But for emotional reasons, too: imagine a childhood with no memory of a kitchen fragranced with the heady scent of baking? Cliché notwithstanding, it is still one of the best things in life.

It's all very well to be able to conjure up an impressive dinner party once a month, or to reel off what vegetables are in season at any given time. But to me, a kitchen that is baked in is the sign of a real, working kitchen. It is a kitchen that provides both nourishment and succour, that can answer any situation.

Every cook needs to know a handful of baking recipes by heart. These are mine. Once you can throw a cake in the oven without consulting a book, it truly does become quick and easy.

flatbread — This is the bread I most often make at home. The oil is what gives it its slightly flaky texture. If you want to make chapattis instead, replace the flour with plain wholemeal flour and omit the oil.

Great warm with anything sloppy, like dips, curries and stews, to mop up gravy, or just with olive oil and salt.

makes 6 x 10cm round flatbreads

200g strong white flour, plus extra for dusting
⅓ teaspoon fast-action dried yeast
½ teaspoon fine salt

170ml lukewarm water
2 tablespoons olive oil, plus extra for greasing

Combine the flour, yeast and salt in a mixing bowl. Mix the water and oil together in a jug. Slowly add the liquid to the dry ingredients, squidging it together with your fingers as you go.

When all the liquid is incorporated, transfer the dough onto a floured surface and knead it firmly, stretching and massaging it until it becomes smooth and elastic. Set the dough aside, if you have time, in a bowl to rise for 45 minutes (if you don't you can go straight on, the breads will just be a little less light).

Knock the air out of the dough by giving it a quick knead, then divide into 6 balls, each about the size of a golf ball. Roll out the balls on a floured surface until they are about 3mm thick. Heat a small, non-stick frying pan over a high heat and cook each bread for 2–3 minutes on each side until just tinged with gold.

Eat as soon as you can, but within 12 hours.

no-knead bread – This bread recipe, from Sullivan Street Bakery in downtown New York, makes the simplest, most delicious homemade bread I have ever tasted. It goes with pretty much everything – it will suit for 'crusty' or 'chewy' bread and is as close as you can get to sourdough without the faff of a starter. You will need to start the night before.

makes 1 x 23cm round loaf
you will need a 23cm cast-iron or ceramic pot with a lid

430g strong white flour
¼ teaspoon fast-action dried yeast
1¼ teaspoons salt

Olive oil, for brushing
Extra flour, for dusting
Polenta (optional)

Mix the flour, yeast and salt together in a mixing bowl. Add 345ml water and mix together with a wooden spoon for 1 minute until you have a shaggy dough.

Lightly coat the inside of a second medium bowl with olive oil and place the dough in the bowl. Cover the bowl with clingfilm and let the dough rest for 12–18 hours at room temperature.

Remove the dough from the bowl and fold it once or twice. Let the dough rest for 15 minutes in the bowl or on the work surface.

Next, shape the dough into a ball. Generously coat a tea towel with flour or polenta, and place the dough seam-side down on the towel. Dust with flour. Cover the dough with a tea towel and let it rise for 1–2 hours at room temperature, until it has more than doubled in size.

Preheat the oven to 230°C/gas 8, placing the cooking pot inside.

Once the dough has more than doubled in size, remove the pot from the oven and place the dough inside the pot, seam-side up. Cover with the lid and bake for 30 minutes. Then remove the lid and bake for a further 15–30 minutes uncovered, until the loaf is nicely browned.

Leave in the pot until it is cool enough to handle – at least 10 minutes. Then turn it out onto a wire rack and let it cool more before you slice it. Best eaten within a couple of days.

victoria sponge — I've used the time-honoured, accurate method for making this cake, by weighing the eggs in their shells (they will be around 240g) and then measuring out exactly the same amount of butter, flour and sugar.

For this cake, you can do whatever you like to sandwich it together — while raspberry jam is the classic filling, whipped cream and fresh raspberries are always a welcome summer alternative.

This is also a great recipe for cupcakes — simply drop spoonfuls of the mixture into paper cases and bake for 8–10 minutes. How you decorate them is up to you — sometimes you want the full buttercream icing extravaganza, at others, a simple dusting of icing sugar is best.

makes 1 x 20cm round cake
you will need 2 x 20cm springform or loose-bottomed tins

Butter, for greasing
4 medium eggs
About 240g butter, softened
About 240g self-raising flour,
   sifted

About 240g caster sugar
2 teaspoons baking powder
Raspberry jam or fresh raspberries
   and whipped cream, to fill
Icing sugar, to dust

Preheat the oven to 180°C/gas 4. Lightly grease the tins and base-line with baking parchment. Weigh the eggs. Measure out exactly the same weight in butter, flour and sugar.

Place the butter and sugar in a large mixing bowl and beat them together — an electric beater of some kind really helps — until pale and fluffy. This will take 10 minutes or so, but really is worth the effort.

Beat together the eggs and, spoonful by spoonful, incorporate them into the creamed mixture with the electric beater; take it slow or it will curdle. Finally, with a metal spoon, fold in the baking powder and flour, one quarter at a time, until well mixed in, but try not to overwork.

Divide the mixture between the two tins and bake for 25 minutes, until the middle feels springy to the touch. Allow to cool slightly before turning out of the tins, then transfer to a wire rack to cool completely.

Peel off the paper and sandwich the flat sides together with raspberry jam or raspberries and cream. Dust the top with icing sugar.

blueberry muffins — Muffins should be light, soft, damp, fragrant but somehow hearty at the same time.

You can easily adapt this recipe and flavour the muffins according to what you fancy: grated cheese (omitting the sugar, of course), dried or fresh fruit, orange or lemon zest or shards of chocolate all work well. The general rule is that if the additions are fairly dry, such as grated cheese, dried fruit or citrus zest, mix with the dry ingredients, but if they are wet, such as fresh fruit or chocolate, fold in at the end according to the recipe below.

makes 12
you will need a muffin tray and paper muffin cases

1 egg white
1 tablespoon rapeseed oil or other light
  oil (not olive oil)
110ml skimmed milk
20g butter, melted
200g plain flour
1 teaspoon baking powder

¼ teaspoon bicarbonate of soda
¼ teaspoon salt
100g caster sugar (or a bit more if you
  want them to be sweeter or you are
  not using sweet fruit)
140g blueberries

Preheat the oven to 200°C/gas 6. Place 12 paper muffin cases in the tin.

In a large bowl, whisk the egg white with an electric beater until soft peaks form, then gently stir in the oil, milk and melted butter.

In a separate bowl, mix together the flour, baking powder, bicarbonate of soda, salt and sugar. Sift the dry ingredients over the egg white mixture and fold it in – it doesn't matter if the mixture is lumpy, it should be fairly well combined but not overworked. Fold the blueberries into the mixture.

Fill each paper muffin case two-thirds full, then bake for 20–25 minutes until golden brown.

Transfer the muffins to a wire rack to cool. Store in an airtight container for several days.

mini berry fairy cakes — These dinky cakes make lovely petits fours, somehow escaping the tweeness of the iced cupcake.

makes 24
you will need a mini cupcake tray and mini paper cases

150g caster sugar
150g butter, softened
2 eggs, beaten
150g self-raising flour

2–3 tablespoons milk
24 berries, eg raspberries, blueberries
  and blackcurrants
Sieved icing sugar, for dusting

Preheat the oven to 180°C/gas 4.

Place the sugar and butter in a large bowl and cream them together until they are pale and fluffy. Slowly incorporate the eggs, beating well in between each addition.

Fold in the flour with a metal spoon. Add a little milk if necessary for a softly dropping batter. Dot a little of the mixture into each case to half fill, and push in a berry.

Bake for 4–5 minutes until turning golden on top. Allow to cool on a wire rack and dust with icing sugar to serve.

chocolate cake

chocolate cake – This wonderfully textured dark chocolate cake, based on London bakery Konditor and Cook's curly wurly cake, would suit any occasion.

makes 1 x 20cm round cake
you will need 2 x 20cm sandwich tins

for the sponge:
175g plain flour
1 teaspoon baking powder
2 tablespoons cocoa powder
250ml milk
275g soft brown sugar
100g 70% cocoa solids dark chocolate,
  broken into pieces

100g butter, softened
2 eggs, beaten

for the icing:
250g 70% cocoa solids dark chocolate,
  broken into pieces
250ml double cream

Preheat the oven to 190°C/gas 5. Line the sandwich tins with foil. Sieve the flour, baking powder and cocoa powder together into a bowl.

Place half the milk, half the soft brown sugar and the chocolate in a saucepan, and heat gently to melt, stirring constantly to stop the chocolate from setting at the bottom of the pan. Once melted, remove from the heat and leave to cool.

Place the butter and the remaining sugar in a large mixing bowl and, using a hand-held electric mixer, cream them together until light and fluffy. Gradually add the beaten eggs, occasionally adding a few spoons of the sieved flour mixture to stop it from splitting.

Add the rest of the flour and milk, mix well, then add the warm chocolate milk mixture. Mix until smooth, with a runny consistency. Divide between the tins and bake for 20–25 minutes. Remove from the oven and leave to cool in the tins.

Next, make the icing. Place the chocolate and cream in a small pan and heat gently to melt the chocolate. Whisk until you have a smooth, rich cream.

Turn the cakes out of the tins and peel off the foil. Transfer to a wire rack and allow to cool completely.

Sandwich the two sponges together with a little of the icing, then spread a thin layer on the top and sides to bind any crumbs. Leave to set for an hour and then repeat the coating, smoothing with a palette knife. Decorate if you like.

scones — To get scones really light and airy and not biscuity, I find it best to use a food processor – you need to cut the fat into the flour with as little work or warmth as possible, similar to when you are making pastry. If you have good, cold pastry hands, you could rub the fat into the flour instead.

I like to cut the scones out small, using the rim of a Champagne glass as a cutter, so you feel less guilty when you eat two.

makes 8–10

Butter, for greasing
225g self-raising flour
½ teaspoon salt
50g caster sugar
1 teaspoon baking powder
50g chilled butter, cut into pieces

150ml milk
Flour, for dusting
Milk, for brushing
Clotted cream and jam or
  lemon curd, to serve

Preheat the oven to 220°C/gas 7. Grease 2 baking sheets.

Place the flour, salt, sugar and baking powder in a food processor and briefly pulse to combine. Add the butter and whizz for a few blasts until a breadcrumb-like consistency is formed.

Add the milk and very briefly whizz again – you are not looking for a smooth texture, just a soggy mass. Transfer to a floured board and very briefly roll out to a 2cm thickness. Cut with a 5cm round cutter (or a Champagne glass) and put onto the baking sheets.

Brush with the milk and bake for 10–12 minutes until risen and just beginning to turn golden.

Transfer to a wire rack to cool a little.

Eat while still warm if you can, with clotted cream and jam or lemon curd. They will keep for a couple of days in an airtight container, but are best eaten fresh.

toasted sesame flapjacks — These chewy flapjacks are given a new dimension with a hint of sesame. It somehow makes them feel healthier too.

makes 12
you will need a 23cm square baking tin

Butter, for greasing
25g sesame seeds
200g butter
75g condensed milk

175g soft brown sugar
100g golden syrup
1 tablespoon tahini
400g jumbo rolled oats

Preheat the oven to 160°C/gas 3. Line the baking tin with greased baking parchment.

Toast the sesame seeds in a dry frying pan for a few minutes, shaking from time to time, until they begin to colour, then set aside on a cool plate.

Place the butter, condensed milk, sugar, syrup and tahini in a large pan and gently heat together until melted. When you have a smooth liquid, add the oats and toasted seeds and stir until evenly mixed through.

Tip the mixture into the tin and bake for 20–25 minutes until turning golden. Remove from the oven and cut into rectangles whilst still warm. Allow to cool in the tin.

These will keep happily in an airtight lidded container for a week or so.

pistachio cake with lemon icing — This cake is adapted from a much-loved Nigel Slater recipe. It's rich, nutty and scented, and completely beguiling. I have used polenta instead of flour, which gives it a welcome bit of grit. Perfect for pudding (or anytime) with a cup of mint tea.

makes 1 x 20cm round cake
you will need a 20cm springform tin

80g blanched almonds
100g skinned pistachios
225g butter, softened, plus extra
  for greasing
225g caster sugar
3 eggs
Juice of 1 lemon
1 teaspoon rosewater

80g polenta
1 teaspoon baking powder

for the icing:
100g icing sugar, sieved
Juice of 1 lemon
Dried edible rose petals and
  pistachios, to decorate

Preheat the oven to 160°C/gas 3. Grease and base-line the cake tin with a circle of baking parchment.

Gently toast the almonds and pistachios in a dry frying pan until tinged with gold. Transfer to a food processor and grind until fairly fine. They will retain an uneven quality, which is part of the charm and texture of the cake.

Place the butter and sugar in a mixing bowl and beat with an electric whisk until pale and fluffy. Add the eggs to the mixture one at a time, beating in between. Fold in the ground almonds and pistachios. Then stir in the lemon juice and rosewater. Finally, mix together the polenta and baking powder, and fold in. You may need a little water to keep the mixture spoonable. Transfer the mixture to the prepared tin.

Bake for 50 minutes or until the top is golden (you may need to lay over a sheet of baking paper if it looks like it's colouring too fast) and an inserted skewer comes out clean. Allow to cool in the tin before turning out onto a wire rack.

Once cool, make the icing by beating the icing sugar with the lemon juice until smooth, and spread over the cake. Scatter with the rose petals and pistachios to decorate.

rocky road — The marshmallows here are a trashy blow to what can be a fairly grown-up treat, so leave them out if you prefer, or replace with almonds to restore dignity. The key is to cut the fruit and marshmallows up into very small bits, so that you have a smooth, sweet, perfectly chewy finish.

feeds 8
you will need a 23cm round baking tin

250g digestive biscuits
150g butter
200g 70% cocoa solids dark chocolate, broken into pieces
1 tablespoon black treacle

3 tablespoons golden syrup
150g dried apricots, finely chopped
150g sultanas, finely chopped
25g marshmallows, finely chopped
Icing sugar, for dusting

Line the baking tin with baking parchment.

Crush the biscuits to a fine powder in a food processor or bash in a plastic food bag with a rolling pin – don't worry if you have a few small chunks.

Over a low heat, melt the butter in a large saucepan with the chocolate, treacle and golden syrup, being very careful not to burn it. Remove from the heat as soon as you can. Stir it together until smooth.

Stir the biscuit crumbs, fruit and marshmallows into the melted mixture and turn into the baking tin. Chill in the fridge until firm, then dust with icing sugar and cut into squares, fingers or wedges.

This will keep for up to a week in an airtight container (if it hasn't all been eaten on the first day).

walnut and espresso cake — This is a dense, moist, simple

version of coffee and walnut cake, wonderful in flavour but not at all like what you'd find on the WI stand.

makes 1 x 450g loaf
you will need a 450g loaf tin

for the sponge:
Butter, for greasing
Flour, for dusting
225g butter, cubed
225g caster sugar
150g ground walnuts
75g self-raising flour
1 teaspoon baking powder
1 teaspoon fine espresso coffee
  grounds

3 eggs
100ml strong espresso coffee
A slug of coffee liqueur (optional)

for the coffee icing:
1 tablespoon strong coffee
2 tablespoons icing sugar

Preheat the oven to 180°C/gas 4. Grease and flour the loaf tin, shaking off any excess.

Blitz together all the sponge ingredients in a food processor apart from the eggs, strong espresso coffee and liqueur, until smooth. Add the eggs, one at a time, pulsing to absorb and then finally add enough espresso coffee, and liqueur, if using, until you have a soft, dropping consistency, then pour into the prepared tin.

Bake for 50–55 minutes, until the top is golden all over and an inserted skewer comes out clean. Check after 30 minutes – if it seems like the surface is colouring too quickly, gently tuck over a sheet of baking parchment.

Once the cake passes the skewer test, allow it to cool for 15 minutes before releasing it from the tin. Wrap the cake in foil and leave it to sit smugly and improve for a day if you have the time.

If you'd like to ice the cake, mix the strong coffee and icing sugar together and spread over the surface of the cake or simply dust with a little sieved icing sugar.

malted date and banana loaf

malted date and banana loaf — This is a dark and sticky but still springy concoction that falls somewhere between a bread and a cake. It has all the gooey goodness of dates without the rich butteriness of a cake, so can be eaten as well for breakfast as for tea.

makes 1 x 450g loaf
you will need a 450g loaf tin

200g medjool dates
Boiling water, for soaking
225g self-raising flour
Pinch salt
1 teaspoon baking powder
½ teaspoon bicarbonate
  of soda
½ teaspoon cinnamon

Handful of sultanas
Handful of walnuts,
  chopped
85g unsalted butter, plus
  extra for spreading
100g soft dark muscovado
  or demerara sugar
100g black treacle

1 tablespoon malt extract
100ml milk
1 ripe banana, mashed
  (optional)
1 egg, lightly beaten

Preheat the oven to 180°C/gas 4. Line the loaf tin with baking parchment.

Remove the date stones, place the dates in a small bowl and just cover them with boiling water. Allow to stand for 5 minutes, then mash until more or less smooth.

Meanwhile, into a large, wide bowl, sieve together the flour, salt, baking powder, bicarbonate of soda and cinnamon. Stir in the sultanas and walnuts.

In a small pan, gently warm together the butter, sugar, treacle, malt extract and dates. Don't let it get too hot; you should be able to hold your finger in it. Remove the pan from the heat, and stir in the milk and banana, if using.

Mix the wet mixture into the dry ingredients and stir everything together thoroughly, ensuring there are no lumps. Finally stir in the egg.

Pour the batter into the prepared tin and bake for about 1 hour or until an inserted skewer comes out clean. Allow to cool a little in the tin before removing, then transfer to a wire rack.

Either eat still warm with a little butter or cool and wrap in foil and store in an airtight container for up to a week.

wholesome chocolate chip cookies — These cookies are
relatively wholesome and are made with brown sugar and brown flour (or a
mixture of white and wholemeal). They will be soft when you remove them
from the oven, but will become deliciously chewy once cool.

makes about 15

125g unsalted butter
175g soft light brown sugar
1 egg, lightly beaten
1 teaspoon vanilla extract
150g wholemeal self-raising flour, or
  100g white flour, 50g wholemeal flour
  and ½ teaspoon baking powder mixed
  together

Pinch salt
100g milk, white or dark chocolate
  chips, or slabs broken into small,
  chip-sized pieces

Preheat the oven to 190°C/gas 5. Line 2 baking sheets with baking parchment.

Melt the butter in a small pan. Place the sugar in a large bowl, add the melted
butter and beat well with a wooden spoon. Beat in the egg and vanilla. Stir in
the flour and salt. Finally mix in the chocolate chips.

Using a dessertspoon, dot spoonfuls of the mixture onto the baking sheets,
leaving 4cm between each, as they will spread. Bake for 8–10 minutes, until
lightly golden, then remove from the oven.

Allow to cool for a couple of minutes on the baking sheets, then transfer to a
wire rack to cool completely.

Store in an airtight container for up to 5 days.

sides and sauces

french beans with lardons

Top the beans, and boil in salted water until just tender. Fry smoked lardons in olive oil until golden, then toss with the beans including the fat from the pan. To make it into a salad, add a splash of white wine vinegar and a good dose of Dijon mustard.

creamed spinach

Bring spinach (fresh or frozen) to the boil and drain, pressing out the liquid with a paper towel. Add a splash of double cream or crème fraîche, a little grated nutmeg, and plenty of salt and pepper. If you want it to be more substantial and soothing, and you can be bothered, make a béchamel to mix it with instead of the cream.

sautéed spinach

Press a clove of garlic under the blade of a knife, and fry in olive oil for a minute or so. Take three times the amount of washed (or defrosted) spinach you think you need and fry, turning, until it wilts and collapses. Serve with a little extra olive oil, a squeeze of lemon, and a pinch of sea salt.

white bean purée

Bring any tinned white beans (haricots, butter or cannellini) in their own water to the boil with a little tomato purée and a very little finely chopped rosemary and garlic, and simmer gently for 10 minutes. Drain, add enough good chicken stock and a dose of best olive oil to make a thick purée and blend. Great with any meat and particularly lamb, on toast, or loosened further with chicken stock and scattered with Parmesan and more olive oil for a hearty soup.

broccoli with olive oil and lemon

Blanch broccoli florets in boiling, salted water for a couple of minutes, then drain. Plunge immediately in cool water to stop the cooking. Drain and dress with best olive oil, lemon juice, and sea salt. This is just as good served warm as at room temperature.

oriental roast butternut with seeds

Cube butternut and roast in olive oil and salt at 180°C/gas 4 for 30 minutes, turning from time to time, until golden and tender. Throw some pumpkin seeds into the dish for the last 5 minutes. Dress with a little finely chopped garlic and grated fresh root ginger and soy sauce. Serve as a side, or on a bed of rocket, as a warm salad.

lentil and herb salad

Toss cooked Puy lentils (the vacuum-packed ones are fine) with chopped, soft-leaf herbs: parsley, mint, dill, whatever takes your fancy. Dress with olive oil, sherry vinegar and Dijon mustard and don't be shy of the salt and pepper. To make more substantial, toss in lardons and their cooking juices.

good old green salad

Choose your lettuce according to your mood or the season and try one of the following:

Cucumber and avocado

Combine the lettuce leaves with very thin slices of peeled cucumber and a chopped, ripe avocado. Dress with olive or rapeseed oil, beaten furiously with white wine or cider vinegar, a dollop of Dijon mustard, and sea salt.

Fresh herb and lemon

Chop about 80g of fresh, green herbs: choose from parsley, mint, chervil, dill, tarragon and basil. Toss the herbs and lettuce together with a simple dressing of lemon juice, best olive oil and crunchy sea salt.

zingy slaw

Shred white cabbage and toss with coriander leaves and lime juice, and a splash of soy sauce and nam pla if you like. Scatter with roasted, salted peanuts smashed with a pestle and mortar.

perfect baked potatoes

Preheat the oven to 200°C/gas 6. For evenly sized, medium to large potatoes, pierce all over with a fork and place in the oven to bake for 60–75 minutes. Do not, under any circumstances, open the oven door, take them out or reduce the temperature until you are absolutely ready to eat, or the perfectly crispy skins will shrivel.

rustic chips

Chop unpeeled potatoes into 1cm sticks. Toss with olive oil, sprinkle with salt, and roast at 220°C/gas 7 for 30–40 minutes, turning every so often.

smooth mash

Boil peeled, floury potatoes (eg King Edward, Desiree or Maris Piper) in lightly salted water until soft, drain and return to the pan, allowing excess water to steam off. Bring a pan of rich whole milk (or add single cream to milk) just to the boil, and add to the potatoes, about 100ml per 500g potatoes. Add a knob of salted butter and beat with a hand-held whisk until completely smooth.

sautéed potatoes

Peel, slice and boil potatoes until nearly cooked. While they're boiling, gently fry chopped onion in olive oil until soft and transparent, and set aside in a bowl. Drain the potatoes and let them stand for a couple of minutes to dry off. Heat a couple more tablespoons of oil until very hot, add the potatoes and fry over a medium-high heat until crisped up – it will take longer than you think. Add the onions for the last few minutes, fry until everything is golden and eat straight away.

minted tahini sauce

Put equal amounts of tahini and water (a few tablespoons should do it), along with a pinch of salt and a little pounded garlic into a bowl, and beat with a whisk or blend with a hand-held electric blender until it emulsifies. Add extra water if necessary, until you have the consistency of double cream. Taste for seasoning and mix in some finely chopped fresh mint. Excellent with lamb, chicken or fish, or just as a dip.

classic pesto

In a food processor, pulse a large bunch of basil with a good handful each of pine nuts and Parmesan, and a fat clove of garlic squashed first under the blade of a knife. Add olive oil while the machine is running until you have a spoonable but soft consistency. Transfer to a jar and seal with a slick of olive oil.

salsa verde

Put into the bowl of a food processor the leaves of a large bunch of parsley and half that amount of mint leaves, adding a little of any other soft herbs you like: tarragon, dill, chervil or oregano. Include capers, anchovy fillets and Dijon mustard, and process until finely chopped. Slowly pour in good-quality olive oil while the machine is running until you have a loose but spoonable consistency. Season with sea salt, and keep in the fridge covered with a slick of olive oil.

real life scenarios

Here are some suggestions for using these recipes in 'Real Life' situations. A board of charcuterie with cornichons, olives and perhaps a bowl of nuts or good crisps will almost always work as a starter. After a big Sunday lunch, or a treatsome supper, I tend to serve a couple of large hunks of cheese on a board before pudding, along with crackers and a green salad (on the same plate, very French, saves on washing up). Cold fruit puddings tend to come with cream, hot, with ice cream, and chocolate with crème fraîche. For scenarios involving children, plain steamed or boiled buttered vegetables such as broccoli, green beans, carrots or peas seem to go down best, along with batons of raw peeled carrots and cucumber, and cherry tomatoes if you want to cover all bases.

brunch and lunch

hearty spring lunch on a cold day
No-knead bread (p.247)
Sausage with chilli and purple sprouting broccoli (p.42)
Rhubarb, Pernod and vanilla compote (p.235)

vegetarian summer brunch
Spring onion, herb and goats' cheese tart (p.211)
Avocado mash on toast (p.130)
Blueberry muffins (p.251)
Roasted peaches (p.214)

summer-ish sunday lunch party
Rosemary Arab breads (p.242)
Rare beef fillet with horseradish sauce (p.166)
Salsa verde (p.273)
Good old green salad with fresh herbs and lemon (p.271)
Scented Eton mess (p.230)

easy-going autumnal lunch
Ed's warm salad (p.51)
Quick raspberry tart (p.214)

a stylish barbecue
Flatbread (p.245)
Spiced butterflied leg of lamb with cucumber raita (p.191)
Minted tahini sauce (p.273)
Lentil, tenderstem broccoli and goats' cheese salad (p.197)
Beetroot, mozzarella and basil salad (p.186)
Good old green salad with fresh herbs and lemon (p.271)
Simple pear custard tart (p.217)

family picnic
Rustic chorizo tortilla (p.92)
Garlic lamb cutlets with houmous (p.78)
Farfalle with broad beans and feta (p.65)
Toasted sesame flapjacks (p.258)

make-ahead weekend lunch for many
Twice-baked cottage pie (p.149)
Broccoli with olive oil and lemon (p.270)
Simple pear custard tart (p.217)

a family sunday lunch
Smoky butternut soup (p.58)
Garlic and thyme roast chicken (p.164)
Perfect baked potatoes (p.272)
French beans with lardons (p.270)
Apple crumble (p.218)

christmassy gathering
Baked Vacherin with truffled almond
    crust (p.112)
Honey rose ham (p.173)
White bean purée (p.270)
Good old green salad (p.271)
Eastern trifle (p.220)

tea

a tea for unruly under tens
Spaghetti with Many veg Bolognese (p.81)
Rocky road (p.262)

elegant tea party
Ripe tomato and Serrano ham on toast (p.108)
Pistachio cake with lemon icing (p.261)
Strawberries in elderflower cordial (p.214)

a very welcome high-tea
St John rarebit (p.52)
Malted date and banana loaf (p.265)
Scones (p.256)
Roasted plums (p.214)

kids' birthday tea
Israeli houmous (p.94)
Sticky garlic drumsticks (p.89)
Sausage burgers (p.78)
Chocolate cake (p.254)
Mini berry fairy cakes (p.253)

supper

comforting tv supper
Potato, fontina and thyme pizzas (p.139)
Greek yoghurt with rosewater, honey,
    pistachios and sultanas (p.214)

supper from store-cupboard heaven
Chicken and spinach rice (p.35)
Greek yoghurt with rosewater, honey,
    pistachios and sultanas (p.214)

sunday evening supper with young kids
Cauliflower cheese with bacon and
    breadcrumbs (p.145)
Apple crumble (p.218)

relaxed dinner party
Spaghetti with Classic pesto (p.273)
Chicken piri piri (p.32)
Sautéed spinach (p.270)
Good old green salad (p.271)
Rose truffles (p.239)

an elegant midweek supper with friends
Rosemary Arab breads (p.242)
Paddy's pork tenderloin with fennel (p.124)
Good old green salad (p.271)
Daisy's molten chocolate puds (p.227)

friday night à deux
Vitello limone (p.122)
French beans with lardons (p.270)
Smooth mash (p.272)
Roasted peaches (p.214)
Wholesome chocolate chip cookies (p.266)

summery saturday dinner party
Club 55 tomato salad (p.194)
Baked sea trout with hazelnuts and samphire
　(p.198)
Good old green salad (p.271)
Sweet fennel tarte tatin (p.232)

**early summer treat (when you'd rather
be on holiday)**
Parma ham with elderflower poached rhubarb
　and burrata (p.111)
Pan-roast pollack with tomatoes, anchovies
　and capers (p.200)
Mini berry fairy cakes (p.253)

high-summer supper
Mackerel Niçoise (p.71)
Susie Brooke's cherry compote with chocolate
　ice cream (p.234)

grown-up midweek birthday supper
Steak with blackened spring onions (p.126)
Sautéed potatoes (p.272)
Good old green salad (p.271)
Cheat's ice cream cake (p.214)
Strawberries in elderflower cordial (p.214)

multigenerational gathering
Lamb stew with tomatoes, chickpeas and
　rice (p.158)
Good old green salad (p.271)
Wholesome chocolate chip cookies (p.266)
Cheat's ice cream cake (p.214)

**gluten- and dairy-free dinner (but not
so that you'd notice)**
Anchovy and oregano chicken and chips
　(p.36)
Broccoli with olive oil and lemon (p.270)
Baked figs with honey and Marsala (p.214)

an elegant vegetable spread
Vegetable stew with saffron and parsley
　pistou (p.162)
No-knead bread (p.247)
Chickpea and feta salad (p.156)
Good old green salad (p.271)
Plum and Sauternes jelly (p.224)

wintry weekend supper with friends
Slow-cooked beef shin stew (p.161)
Perfect baked potatoes (p.272)
Good old green salad (p.271)
Chocolate and hazelnut meringue brownie
　cake (p.223)

directory

nealsyarddairy.co.uk
For the best British artisanal cheese, as well as large chunks of Parmesan.

wellhungmeat.com
Top quality, online butcher, who pays special attention to the provenance and hanging of all meat. Good-value monthly boxes as well as individual orders.

farmison.com
Unusual cuts of meat, rare breed meat and artisanal cheeses.

japanesekitchen.co.uk
Reliable supplier of quality Japanese products.

valvonacrolla.co.uk
Delicatessen with particular focus on excellent Italian products.

riverford.co.uk
Organic general shop and greengrocer, most famous for monthly fruit and veg boxes. Also supplies good deli products, meat and dairy (and even artisanal breads in most of the south).

melburyandappleton.co.uk
Excellent general deli, but also has a good selection of Middle Eastern products such as dried rose petals, pomegranate molasses, flower waters, and sumac.

spiceshop.co.uk
For spices, herbs and a good selection of chillies.

nakedwines.co.uk
Supplier of small but very good quality and value independent wine labels.

acknowledgements

Thank you to …

Richard Atkinson, encourager, enabler and ruthless prose chopper, for the hand-holding and the chilli jam, I am lucky to have you. Natalie Hunt for getting us all in shape, seeing it through with tireless attention to detail and ensuring it looks so beautiful. Jill Mead for gorgeous photos and fun days making them. Georgia Vaux for the brilliant design. All the team at Bloomsbury, in particular Xa Shaw Stewart, Penny Edwards, Alice Shortland, Jane Bamforth, Sally Somers, Tess Viljoen, Sue Pearce and Jude Drake.

Tif Loehnis, for being the best agent imaginable (and having beautiful plates). Rosemary Scoular and Wendy Millyard for picking me up where you left off. Mary Norden, my wise and inspiring editor at *Red*. Claire Bowman, Shaun Phillips and especially Sacha Bonsor (for use of the shoebox and so much more) at *The Times* for all your support.

On the food side, Emily Morley, for cooking patiently and perfectly from chaotic scraps of paper, and always turning out food that looks and tastes lovely, and Sue Henderson for getting us started. Ailana Kamelmacher for your invaluable advice.

On the home front, my sisters: Kate, for taking the prose and patiently sieving it till smooth, I would be stuck on the first chapter without you. Sam, for being an inspiring cook, and food conversationalist, my greed is mostly your fault. Their husbands James Harding and Mark Fletcher, for not remarking on the phone bills.

Daisy Garnett, thank you for being there every step of the way, for the first cook-off, the faultless testing, and for sharing your kitchen and secrets with me in so many ways. Thanks to all my recipe givers and testers including Alex Datnow, Susannah and Pev Hooper, Katherine van Tienhoven, Heather Fleming (brilliant neighbour), Henry McMicking, Julian Kingsland, Charles Cumming (if you want a recipe title next time, start working on it), Bridget Harrison, Melinda Langlands Pearse, Elizabeth Sheinkman, Nixie Graham,

Tom Bartlett, Paddy Sutton, Claire Conrad, Tommy Always, Ruth Rogers, Susie Brooke, Lucinda Garthwaite, Otto Bathurst, Toby Ingram, Dee Pinsent. Anyone who experienced one of the 'meals of many puddings' or whatever else was thrown randomly at your plate in the name of research. If I haven't named you, I still mean to thank you.

Ewelina Brzezinska, Sarah Dawkins and Monika Mucha for looking after the kids so brilliantly.

And finally, Ed. Sweetheart, thank you for supporting me, encouraging me and occasionally attempting to remedy my shocking time management. The enthusiasm with which you bite great chunks out of life is a great inspiration to me. I wouldn't, and couldn't, do any of this without you. Just think of the leftovers.

index